Tricks for Good Grades

Strategies to Succeed in School

Ron Kurtus

SfC Publishing Co.
Lake Oswego, Oregon

Copyright © 2009 by Ron Kurtus
Printed in the United States of America

All rights reserved. No part of this book may be reproduced without written permission of the author, except for the inclusion of brief quotations for reviews or articles.

SfC Publishing Co.
www.sfcpublishing.com

ron.kurtus@sfcpublishing.com

Edited by Carol L. Larson
carol@larson-tech.com

Library of Congress Control Number 2007900220

Kurtus, Ron
    Tricks for Good Grades: Strategies to Succeed in School

    1. Study Skills 2. Education 3. Reference

ISBN 978-0-9767981-0-1

Tricks for Good Grades

Good grades are important
for feeling good about yourself,
being respected by others and
in getting a good job later on in life.

But more important than the grades
is the knowledge that you hope to
gain and retain.

Contents

Section 1	*Introduction*	*1*
Section 2	*Good Grades*	*3*

Factors in Determining Good Grades 5
Cheating to Get a Better Grade. 9
Feedback on Cheating 13

Section 3	*Doing Homework*	*25*

Zip through Homework 27
Get Homework Done 31
Doing Homework with Friends 33
Feedback on Homework. 37

Section 4	*Taking Tests*	*45*

Be Good at Taking Tests 47
Practice Taking Tests. 51
Preparation Needed to Excel in Tests. 53
Mental Process in Preparing for a Test 57
Avoiding Goofing Up Tests 61

Tricks for Good Grades

Contents

Feedback on Tests 65

Section 5 *Teachers* *73*

When the Teacher is a Jerk 75
Getting a Good Teacher 79
Feedback on Teachers 83

Section 6 *Special Skills* *91*

Special Homework Skills 93
Reading Faster 95
Feedback on Reading 99
Speak to Your Class with Confidence 107
Feedback on Speaking 113

Section 7 *Learning and Teaching* *127*

Learn to Get Good Grades by Observing Others 129
Get Better Grades by Teaching Others 133

Section 8 *Personal Improvement* *137*

Achieving Your Goals 139
Being Healthy 145
Feedback on Health 149
Being Knowledgeable 151
Being Excellent 153
Feedback on Excellence 155
Good Character 167
Being Valuable 171
Characteristics of Hyperactive Students 175
Harness Your Hyperactivity 177
Feedback on Hyperactivity 185

Section 9 *Summary* *189*

Ron Kurtus 191

Section 1 — Introduction

Do you want to get better grades in school? Do you want to be able to quickly learn things, so you have more time for enjoyment? Do you want to feel great about yourself in the process, like a champion?

This book is meant for you
Go through the lessons in this book to find helpful methods and tips on doing well in school. They will help you get more out of your school experience.

The goal of this book is to design champions. We want to see you become a leader, a winner, and a success in school and in life.

Sections of the book
The book is divided into several sections or areas of interest.

Good grades
The first area explains the basics of getting good grades. It also points out the pros and cons of cheating to get better grades. Opinions of various students are included to show what other kids think.

Introduction

Doing homework
Homework is a major time-consumer in school. We advocate zipping through your homework and not trying to watch television or talk on the phone at the same time. There are some good techniques that will help you complete your homework.

Taking tests
Test scores are a major part of your final grade in a class. Learning to effectively take tests and exams is a skill that every student wanting better grades should learn. There are a number of important factors and ideas to improve your test-taking abilities explained in this section.

Teachers
There are good teachers and some bad teachers in every school. Hopefully, you don't get stuck with a bad or even mean teacher. But if you do, you need to learn to handle the situation. We give some good tips on how to do that.

Special skills
Being able to give presentations and ways to increase your learning skills are also explained.

Personal improvement
Finally, there are philosophies of personal improvement that are worth noting. These philosophies are the basis of the *School for Champions* and can be applied to everyone seeking success.

Become a top student
Hopefully, this book will guide you to be a top student. You want to do as well as you can in school and become a champion in the process.

Section 2 — **Good Grades**

Getting good grades is what it's all about. But of course, you really want to learn things that are useful in your life. There are some basic factors involved in getting good grades. Although some students try to bypass the requirements and cheat to get better grades, that route usually results in a dead-end.

Chapters in this section:

1. Factors in Determining Good Grades
2. Cheating to Get a Better Grade
3. Feedback on Cheating

Factors in Determining Good Grades

The idea of grading students is to show how well they are learning the subject matter material. Grading is usually a comparison with other students in the class or school, but there is a movement to make a National Standard that everyone should reach.

There are three major factors that determine what sort of grade you will get: test scores, homework, and teacher-student relationship. To get good grades, you must excel in all three areas.

Test scores

The greatest part of your grade is determined from the scores you get in quizzes and tests. If you know the material and are good at taking tests, this should be no problem. However, if you have trouble working under the pressure and time constraints of a test, you may not do well—even if you know the material.

If you want to get good grades in school, it is well worth your while to learn to be good in taking tests. You can often learn to do well in tests by practicing working under the pressure of a taking a test. Of course, you must also have good study habits in being able to learn the material.

Homework

Many teachers grade your homework and make those scores part of your final grade. There are other teachers who just collect the homework and check it over without giving individual grades for the work done.

Good Grades

Important in learning
The reason to do homework is because it is the method used to learn 70% of the subject matter material. The other 30% of the subject matter is learned in class. The percentages vary according to the teacher and subject matter. However, you can see that if you don't pay attention in class, you must depend much more on your homework. If you don't do your homework, your chances of passing any tests or exams are lessened.

Some can fake it
There are students who are good at taking tests and have enough general knowledge that they can get away with not paying attention and not really studying, but yet they can pass the tests. Unfortunately, sooner or later the lack of learning catches up to them, such that they will have trouble figuring out how much to charge for a "Happy Meal" with an extra order of fries.

Do homework effectively
Since homework is a large factor in going to school, you want to learn to do it effectively. Furthermore, since homework can be so time-consuming, you need to know how to get it done in the shortest possible time.

Teacher relationships
Although teachers are supposed to grade purely on your test scores and homework grades, many teachers add their personal feelings to the grade.

A teacher who likes you or is impressed by what you do will often give you extra consideration in grading you. On the other hand, if the teacher does not like you, feels you are disruptive or even disagrees with some views you may have, the teacher may lean the other way and give you a lower grade than is deserved.

Such grading is not fair. Similar unfairness happens to people in their jobs, concerning raises and promotions. That is why it is important to avoid rubbing your teacher the wrong way or getting on the wrong side of the teacher.

If you want decent grades from the teacher, it is worthwhile to be cordial and respectful, even if you don't like him or her.

Summary

If you want to get good grades in school, it is important to learn how to take tests. Homework can be time-consuming, but it is important in learning and being able to pass tests, so you need to learn to do your homework effectively. Teachers are human and may be prejudiced. Since they have the power to determine your grade, it is wise to treat them with respect.

Cheating to Get a Better Grade

You can get better grades by cheating. But is it worth it? You may be under pressure to get good grades in school that cause you to consider cheating on your homework and tests. If you cheat but are lucky enough not to get caught, you may get the good grades you seek.

However, being caught cheating may also result in being expelled from school. Plus, there are the long-term consequences of not learning and moral decline. It is a decision you must make.

Pressure to cheat

Parents often pressure their children to get good grades. If their boy or girl doesn't reach a certain level of expectation, the parents may reprimand, punish or ground the student. Therefore, the students may cheat to simply to satisfy their parents' expectations.

Sometimes students neglect to do their homework or to study for a test. Sometimes they are too busy or forgot to do the work. However, more often it is because the students just didn't feel like doing the work. So to avoid doing the work involved and not let anyone know they goofed off, students will copy someone else's homework or test answers.

Pros and cons of cheating

You may be able to get good grades through cheating, but also you may be caught.

Benefits of cheating

If you copy the work of others—whether it is plagiarizing material from books or the Internet or copying the homework of another student—it results in not having to work very hard for a passing or even good grade. Cheating is like getting something for nothing.

In fact, in some colleges, there are people who sell homework and test answers. They make money and the student gets a good grade with little work. Everyone thinks he or she is happy.

Consequences of cheating

Being caught cheating on a test or copying someone else's material for homework can result in a lowered grade and even expulsion from school. If you don't get caught, there is still the problem that you haven't learned the material. That ignorance may come to haunt you down the road, when you are required to apply what you've learned.

In either case, there is also the moral stigma that you subconsciously hold inside of you that you didn't deserve the grade you received and that you are a cheater. Such a person may go far in life, but he or she will never be a champion.

Dumb cheater

There is a story about how Johnny didn't study for his math test, but he sat right next to Mary, who was the smartest kid in class. He decided to use a mirror so he could see her paper and copy her answers. Unfortunately, he copied all the answers backwards. She got a 94 on the test, but he only got a 49. (The grade was backwards too!)

Cheating mother

A high school teacher I know said he received a term paper from a female student who had obviously copied material from a book word-for-word. After the teacher failed the student, her mother

Cheating to Get a Better Grade

called and demanded he give her daughter a top grade, so she could go on to a good college. The mother saw nothing wrong with cheating, as long as her daughter got top grades.

Hopefully, you don't have a mother like that.

What should you do?

Suppose your parents would like you to get good grades in a class, but you just don't understand the material or maybe you had missed some assignments and weren't ready for the final exam. Also, suppose you had an opportunity to get the answers to the test ahead of time. Should you cheat?

This is a dilemma. On one hand, if you take the test and try to do your best, you may fail or get a poor grade. But on the other hand, if you cheat, you can be sure that you will pass with a good grade. And the chances of getting caught are slim.

The best bet is to take the test and do as well as you can. If you don't pass or receive a good grade, so be it. You can't make believe you are what you aren't. And besides, even if you get away with cheating once, it just isn't worth the risk.

Summary

Although you may be pressured by your parents to get good grades, you should not cheat on homework or tests. If you claim to be too lazy to do the work or are looking for an easy way out, cheating is not the solution.

You may gain in the short-term with good grades, but in the end you will lose out. If you are caught cheating, you may be punished and perhaps kicked out of school. At the very least, you will be stigmatized as someone that can't be trusted. If you don't get caught, you will probably end up lacking needed knowledge and skill. You might also become morally bankrupt. Don't cheat!

Realize that you have the potential to get good grades without cheating.

Feedback on Cheating

Students from around the world send email to the *School for Champions* with questions and comments on various aspects of getting good grades in school. The following letters concern cheating in school. Note that the letters have not been edited for correct grammar or spelling.

Give me good reasons why I shouldn't cheat

Question
November 7

In my school not only do most kids cheat on most tests but they cheat on the SATS as well. I'm talking about major cheating usually 30% of the test and they never get caught because the teachers don't care. These kids for the most part get much better grades than the non-cheaters do and do much better on their SATS and get into a better college. Give me one good reason why I shouldn't cheat.

(no name given) - **USA**

Answer
Who is worse: The teachers who don't care and allow cheating or the kids who take advantage and cheat?

Those teachers who don't want to bother to do a good job in teaching students and in monitoring their behavior should be fired from their jobs! They are hurting all the students by their negligence, as well as wasting the hard-earned money that the parents are paying to educate their kids.

Good Grades

It makes it tough on you to have to try to compete for good grades against other students who are cheating. But note that once the cheaters get to college the game gets much harder. They have missed out on needed knowledge, since they've gotten by through cheating. Also, if they try to continue to cheat and get caught in college, they probably will have to face dire consequences.

Look at it this way: If you would cheat, would you feel good about yourself? If you cheated and got an A, would you feel as good as if you didn't cheat and got a B that you deserved? Another thought is: Suppose you would cheat and just your luck, you are the only one who is caught. Would it be worth it?

I think it is better to be able to walk tall and know you did the best you could. It is also good to realize that you know the class materials, while the cheaters probably don't.

If it were my choice, I would take the high road instead of the low road.

I like cheating

Question
October 30

Hey Dude, I like cheating. It's way cool man!

(no name given) - **Australia**

Answer
Yes, it is fun to cheat when you can get away with it. One problem is if you get caught and must pay the consequences. You could fail or get kicked out of school. But even if you don't get caught, you really are robbing yourself by not learning what you need to know.

I think it's cooler to show how good you really are.

Feedback on Cheating

Disagrees on views of cheating

Question
September 7

I am not a cheat, nor do I condone the practice. However, in your valiant attempt to put an end to it, you have been issuing false statements doubtless formed by plain old common sense.

In many of your responses, you've said that cheaters in one area of their life become cheaters in other areas (marriages, taxes, etc.). As a matter of fact, even cheaters in one area of *school* don't become cheaters in another. In studies by psychologists, it was discovered that some students cheated on math or English or P.E. when given certain tasks to carry out and then being watched to see if they reported results correctly, but not on all of them. Cheating depends on the subject and the environment.

Even personality traits don't carry over from one area of your life to others. It was previously assumed that older children in families were more domineering in their lives, and the younger children were more rebellious. This assumption may be true in the family sense, but in other environments (work, school, play) it doesn't make any difference and has no scientific validity whatsoever.

Cheating in one area is not contagious, and will not make you less trustworthy to your friends and lovers. Some people might be quiet at school but animated and charismatic with their friends, or vice versa, and some may be slippery and untrustworthy to their coworkers (or classmates) but fiercely loyal to friends.

You will argue and use soothing words and eventually come back to the same conclusion as in every letter, and you will make yourself seem the wiser and above my intellectual level as if I was just curious and seeking your advice rather than arguing on an equal basis, and you will calmly "thank me for my opinion."

Good Grades

But I have a point and you cannot debate its validity.

(no name given) - **The Galactic Empire**

Answer
"Common sense" is usually based on the common experience of many people. But it is possible that it does not cover all cases. Studies by psychologists certain give us some insight on the basis of cheating. But it is necessary to compare the views of many psychologists and behaviorists to get closer to a true model of human behavior.

Some people will cheat in school or elsewhere only a few times out of desperation, opportunity or such. They may go on through their lives as relatively honest people. I agree that in many situations, a person may cheat depending on the subject and environment. But it also is a character issue. Cheating does not only depend on the subject and environment. Some people are just more honest (or dishonest) than others.

If a friend cheats at school or steals from someone else, you may still trust him in your personal relationship. But if he cheats, lies or steals from you, the odds are that you will not completely trust him again, even if he was your best friend.

This is a complex subject, as is any topic on human behavior. I certain welcome debate and feel your views have some validity.

Should I tell the teacher?

Question
September 7

If half the class is cheating, and the teacher then leaves the room, when the teacher comes back, should you tell the teacher in front of the class or in private or not at all?

(no name given) - **USA**

Feedback on Cheating

Answer
You don't want to tell in front of the class, because everyone will be down on you. Leaving the situation alone isn't good, because it indirectly affects your grade.

It is best to let the teacher know in private. Say, "I just wanted to let you know that I think some students are cheating when you leave the room." Then if the teacher asks who is cheating, you can say, "I can't say it for sure, so I don't want to wrongly accuse any individual." In this way, you aren't a squealer, but you still let the teacher know of the problem.

Hopefully, the teacher will not spot you out in front of the class as "the honest student."

I hope these ideas help in a sticky problem.

I'm a cheater

Question
April 18

I'm a cheater. I admit it. I have nothing to hide. I read many things about cheating and from all the information I was able to find about cheating I have found one compelling idea. We as human being want to excel. Now we as human beings are very rebellious, countries have gone to rebellion to fight off their evil dictators. This leads to cheating. Why?

Well because we all want to excel. We all want to have the highest grades to enter collage. Now there are two paths to getting good grades. Learning the material and passing the test or taking the path of the outlaw and cheating.

The first method is to spend countless hours learning useless information. Now I know you are going to reply by telling me it's not useless. But if you know you will never use the quadratic equation in your entire life then why learn it?

Good Grades

This leads me to cheat. I know I will never need most of the information provided in school. In my eyes school is a prison to fill my mind with information that I have no desire for. The Teachers are the guards and they are forcing this information into me. When I cheat, I feel like I'm rebelling against this system and telling them that I'm a free person and will not let them waste my time with their knowledge. Because I can spend the time it would of taken to memorize conics by learning something that is really interesting to me.

Now I want to go to the best collage possible. I know that I will have a much higher chance of getting into a collage if I cheat. Now tell me isn't the smart thing to do is to go with the higher chances? Well especially since by taking this method I make it much easier for myself. Why should I listen to the guards in this prison system called school when I can cheat?

(no name given) - **USA**

Answer

First of all, when you cheat in school, you are cheating yourself of an education. How do you know what information is needed after you leave school? How do you know what is needed to get a good job and be able to even hold an intelligent conversation with someone?

You can cheat your way through high school and even through college. But there is a point where the lack information and knowledge you did not bother to learn will come back to hurt you severely.

Another issue is the type of person you are. If you cheat in school, you probably cheat elsewhere. On the other hand, would you like to have your friends cheat you? Would you like to have a loved one pull the wool over your eyes?

What you really need to do is to get good at school. Be good at learning and taking tests, so that it is not a great effort. Be curious about things, whether it is comic books or ancient history. Get your mind to the point where you can suck in information and knowledge and instantly memorize it. And get rid of the attitude that the teachers are forcing things on you. They are just doing their job and trying to educate the students. Some will learn and some are fools. Please don't be a fool.

I hope you look at yourself with pride and set a good example of others. No one likes a cheat. No one!

Why can't students cheat sometimes?

Question
March 2

Is this call cheating when you didn't do your homework or forgot to do it? Then you have to copy off of someone's paper?

Why can't students cheat sometimes, if it is important?

Keisha - **USA**

Answer
What happens if you copy a wrong answer and the teacher sees that two of you have the same wrong answer? Then you are both in trouble and get worse grades.

I am sure the teacher would agree that it is better to say you forgot to do the homework than it is to copy someone else's and say it is yours. You didn't learn anything (which the homework is supposed to help) plus you lied and cheated. Once you get caught cheating like that, the teacher will never trust you and perhaps even keep a close eye on you.

So, you gain in the short run, but you lose more in the long run.

I've cheated on math and don't feel guilty

Question
December 4

I have cheated on math papers and other assignments and I don't feel guilty about it. I do it because my parents put so much pressure on me to get straight A's and because I don't have time to do the homework or because I don't understand the assignment and it is way overdue. Maybe if parents didn't put so much pressure on their kids then their kids wouldn't be forced to cheat.

(no name given) - **USA**

Answer
Your parents put the pressure on you because they want you to excel, so they can be proud of you. Unfortunately, they sometimes don't realize that they are being selfish and causing too much stress in their children.

The thing to consider is what would happen if you were caught cheating? Would your parents be proud or ashamed? Would your teachers trust you again? Would good grades mean anything when others give a bad report on you?

It is not worth the risk.

But what if you never get caught? There will be a point in your life when you suddenly find out that you can't move ahead by cheating, and you haven't learned things you need to know.

The best thing to do is to work on improving your ability to study and learn. Also, try to get your parents to ease off on you. That is not easy to do, but why let them screw up your life?

Feedback on Cheating

Don't want friends to cheat

Question
August 11

I know kids who copy my paper for school, but now that I have read this I don't want them to. I don't want them to be losers in school. Now I'll tell them about your website. It really isn't worth cheating if you don't learn anything.

I know even the smartest girl in class has cheated. She did off my final exam for school. I thought it was an easy exam. If she thought she would need help she should have called someone or asked the teacher. Well anyways, thanks for showing me how bad it is to cheat. I will definitely tell my friends.

Chelsey - **USA**

Answer
It is really a shame that some kids cheat, but they just try the easy way out.

There are two other things wrong with letting others copy from you. One is that you become part of the crime. And if the teacher would catch the cheater, you might be blamed as helping out.

Another problem is that grading is done by comparison or what they call "on a curve." If someone gets a higher grade than he or she deserves, that can actually lower the value of your grade.

Although some may not like the fact that you won't let them copy, you also must look out for yourself by not going along with it.

Best wishes in school, and I hope you get great grades!

Good Grades

Wants to apologize for cheating

Question
May 25

Hi. I have cheated several times and got caught but blamed it on the kid next to me. So what do I, because I want to apologize and tell my teacher how should I tell her?

(no name given) - **San Diego**

Answer
Although it is not good that you cheated, it is good that you feel sorry about it and want to make amends. It would be wonderful for you to tell the teacher and apologize for what you did. I am sure it will make you feel better about the situation.

But you also must consider the consequences of telling the teacher. Plus, if you tell the teacher, your parents will also probably find out that you cheated. It may depend on how they would react.

If your parents would ground you for a while or just scold you, then that would not be too bad. But even if you mean well by apologizing, some parents may overreact. You have to know your parents.

Likewise, if your teacher would accept your apology and warn you not to do it again or perhaps lower your grade a little, it would not be too bad. But some teachers might get very angry and make an example of you. I guess you need to have an idea of how the teacher might respond. Also, what about the kid you blamed? Would he or she be angry at you?

So in other words, if you apologize, you may be punished. But if you don't apologize, it will be on your conscience.

Feedback on Cheating

You will have to use your judgment whether to tell your parents first, tell the teacher first, or just let it pass by. Your apology could be something like, "I want to apologize for something I did that was wrong, and I'm so embarrassed about it. I cheated on a recent test, and I know it wasn't right. I'm very sorry for it and will never do something like that again."

This is difficult advice to give, because I do want you to feel good about yourself, but also I don't want you to get in some serious trouble. At the very least, use the experience as a lesson to never, ever cheat again.

Cheated and now feel guilty

Question
January 8

I've cheated a couple of times and I admit it. Last semester, my speech teacher gave us a study guide before the required final. I love studying for tests, it's just that this semester I have a part-time job and I don't have time to do it. I was prepared for this exam however and the teacher didn't even give me (or any other senior in that class) a chance to prove (at least) myself that I learned what she taught me. She gave us the test, then our blank Scantron and one with the answers so we could pass it around like if we were professionals. I felt like a criminal, and not only like a criminal, but like a mentally handicapped senior. What could I do to raise my own self-esteem and changed my school's morals?

Vicky - **USA**

Answer
There is a great temptation to cheat in school, especially if the teacher makes it easy to do so. It really feels a lot better to prove to yourself how much you know. Even if the grade wasn't as good as you would like, at least it is your grade.

Good Grades

Consider yourself fortunate that you felt guilty about your cheating episode. Some start cheating and they just can't seem to stop until it is too late.

It takes character to realize you have made a mistake, and it is a good lesson to you not to let yourself get sucked into such a situation again. Move on, and if a situation comes up again where cheating is an option, just tell yourself that you have the integrity not to lower yourself. It is better to get a lower grade and feel proud that it is your grade than to get a top grade through cheating.

It is difficult to change other people or institutions. The most you can do is to set a good example yourself. That will certainly build and maintain your self-esteem.

You've got what it takes to be a champion.

Section 3: Doing Homework

Teachers often assign reading, problems and other work to be done at home and turned in the next time the class meets, usually the next day. Some teachers then grade the homework or at least verify that it has been done correctly. The idea of homework is to learn what was briefly covered in class and to do some real-world exercises. Some teachers give a lot of homework, while others give little.

The big problem for students is getting this work done in a limited time. It is sometimes difficult with other activities, including socializing or entertainment. In fact, it takes considerable discipline to get down to several hours of intense homework after a hard day at school and when your friends are calling up and wanting to go hang out.

Chapters in this section:

1. Zip through Homework
2. Get Homework Done
3. Doing Homework with Friends
4. Feedback on Homework

Zip through Homework

Some students seem to spend more time on their homework than they would like to. For them, it seems like it never ends. They feel that homework is a drag and takes much more time from life than it should. Instead, their philosophy should be that they zip through their homework, so they can go out and have fun but still learn the material and get good grades.

Many don't zip
Most students would like to spend less time on their homework but very few actually look into methods that can cut the time spent on it.

Some simply skip their homework and pay the consequences of poor grades and not learning things. Others are so worried about doing well, that they devote their lives to homework instead of being able to go out and have some fun.

You don't want to spend more time than is necessary on homework unless it is something you truly enjoy doing. You want to get through the material in the most effective and efficient ways possible.

Have an attitude of speed
How fast you go through your homework has much to do with your attitude and priorities. You should think in terms of speed and getting the work done, even before you start. The choice is yours whether to spend the whole evening on homework or to get the job done as soon as possible.

Doing Homework

Focus on allotted time
If your goal is to get through with your homework as soon as possible, because you have other things you want to do, then you must set your mind to that goal and focus at completing the task in an allotted time period.

How much time should you spend?
Teachers usually have an idea of how long the homework assignments they give should take you. Some say 1-hour homework per class hour, while other teachers require less time.

Find out what their estimate is. If you are taking much longer than the teacher expects, then it is possible that you are ineffective in your study habits.

Time yourself
Time how long it takes you to do the homework in each subject. By measuring the approximate time it takes, you can tell if you are spending more time than you should on a specific subject.

Use special homework skills
Once you have set your mind to how you are going to do your homework, you get down to the actual task. Homework usually consists of reading material in your textbook and doing written assignments. Sometimes you must do outside research on a subject.

You want to be able to read the material rapidly, understand what you read and remember important points. Then you must answer questions, solve problems or write out reports. You want to go through each area quickly and efficiently. In some areas there are skills to increase your effectiveness.

Get it done

You want to get your homework done as fast as possible. Who wants to spend excess time on homework, when there are other things to do? The way to do get it done is to manage your time, don't get sidetracked, keep focused and switch subjects when saturated.

Summary

You can zip through your homework if you have the proper mindset, use some simple techniques such as reading faster and improving your memory, and focus on finishing your homework.

Get Homework Done

In order to finish your homework as fast as possible, you need to manage your time and make sure you don't become sidetracked. Instead, keep focused on your homework goal and switch subjects when mentally saturated on a specific subject.

Manage your time

Once you get your assignments for the day, you need to make some plans to manage how you will spend your time. Determine how much time you want to spend on homework and if you have other pressing engagements to attend that evening.

Set aside a certain amount of time to do each homework assignment. It is not a bad idea to write down your time schedule.

Then try to blast through each subject, concentrating on getting the job done. In this way you won't dawdle or doodle. If you don't have a time limit set on a subject, you may take longer than necessary to finish your homework.

Don't be sidetracked

If you are trying to finish your homework quickly, don't let yourself be sidetracked by minor distractions. Set aside specific time periods for doing your homework. You can always phone your friend at a different time or during a break.

Keep focused

One thing to do is to concentrate on getting the job done. Unless you have a hyperactive mind, don't try to do several things at once. Rather, focus on getting it done right away, so that you can enjoy some free time.

Listening to music
Many like to listen to music while studying. If it doesn't interfere with your mental concentration, fine. Some students can listen to music while studying, some can't. See what works best for you.

Watching television
Do NOT watch television while doing your homework. It will take you forever to finish your homework, and you will most likely do a poor job at it.

Doing homework with friends
If you are going to do homework with friends, make sure you don't spend too much time goofing around or talking. (See Doing Homework with Friends for more ideas.)

Switch subjects
If you have a lot of homework to do, try switching subjects every 40 minutes or so. If you stay on one subject for too long, you can become mentally saturated and less efficient.

Researchers found that when you become saturated and change to a completely different subject—like from Math to English—you use a different part of your brain. This results in a mental freshness and being able to get more done. Later, you can go back to the original assignment to finish it at that time.

If you pace yourself like this, you will be able to get a lot more done in a shorter span of time. Experiment to see what works best for you.

Summary
Concentrate on getting your homework done by managing your time. Keep focused on your homework goal and don't become sidetracked. Switch to a different subject when you feel mentally saturated.

Doing Homework with Friends

They often say: "Two heads are better than one." Sometimes that can be true when doing your homework. An effective way to work on homework assignments, reports or projects is to do it with friends or fellow classmates. You can often get more done and learn better when you are able to discuss things with another person.

The biggest problem with doing homework or projects together is that it is so easy to start talking about other, more pleasant or fun things. Also, some friends are better as friends than as study-mates. Thus, you should have a good plan of action for studying together.

Check your study methods

You need to determine whether your personality and study methods would work well if you studied with another person.

Solitary studying

Some students prefer to concentrate by themselves when they study. They need to focus on their work in order to get it done or to solve a problem. Disruptions from other people can break their train of thought and make it difficult to get back on track.

Social studying

Other students are more social in their thinking and study styles. They like to play ideas off others and discuss things before putting it down on paper. These are the students who will do well in studying with friends or other students.

Doing Homework

Of course, there is always the temptation to socialize more than to study. With a little planning you can enjoy the company of your friend and still get the homework assignment completed.

Instant messaging
There is also a compromise to this method, where students will be studying alone but will interface through Instant Messaging, email or the telephone. Even the student who prefers to study alone can break his or her concentration to contact a friend and ask for some information.

Work and tests
Note that in the modern office workplace, many companies are emphasizing group projects. Those who prefer to work alone on projects often are told to work in a group.

But also note that students who like to work alone probably will do better in test situations that those who like to study in a social environment.

Know your study partner
It may seem obvious that you know with whom you are studying, but quite often you don't realize the other person's goals, abilities and methods until you start working with him or her. Some friends may be fun but may also inhibit your ability to finish your assignment.

Some friends only goof around
Some people just want to socialize and don't have a goal of really getting anything done. With such a study partner, you might end up not finishing your assignment.

Others may have nothing to contribute or may want you to do all the work for them. The person may be a friend, but who wants to always be doing someone else's work?

Doing Homework with Friends

Be selective
Although it is often fun to work on an assignment or project with others, you also must remember that you have a goal of getting the homework done and receiving a good grade on it. You may need to be selective in finding a study-mate. Unfortunately, the only way to do that is by trial and error.

Plan your activity
When you study alone, you just do it. Perhaps you may set aside a specific time to do your work. However, when you study with friends, you need a definite plan of action concerning a time limit and how much socializing is allowed.

Set a time limit before you start
When you set a time limit on something, you usually will finish it within time. This is true for doing homework, too. Set a time limit to finish the assignment that you and your friend are working on.

For example, you could say, "Let's work together on the History assignment from 8 to 9 PM."

Then you could plan to do other things after the assignment is complete. Amazingly, when you set a time limit on work, you usually can finish it within that time.

Divide projects into parts
A good way of working together is to control the situation by alternating between serious work and conversation.

Divide your project into small parts and set a goal to complete each part, mixing in breaks for enjoyment. Also, setting time limits to complete various parts of your assignment helps to keep the mix of talk and work in the proper perspective.

Wrap it up on time

My feeling is that in any type of activity, when the time is up, you wrap it up. In other words, when you get near the end of a study session, you make quick decisions and finish everything up.

Try to never let loose ends dangle. Finish the job or the part of the task you had planned to finish.

Summary

You can work with friends on assignments to zip through your homework, provided you select good study-mates, you alternate between focused work and breaks and you complete the job in the allotted time. Studying together is one of several strategies you can use to do well in school. See if it will help you become a top student.

Feedback on Homework

Students from around the world send email to the *School for Champions* with questions and comments on various aspects of getting good grades in school. The following letters concern doing homework. Note that the letters have not been edited for correct grammar or spelling.

Don't feel like doing homework

Question
November 22

I donno..i'm in 9th grade now...and everytime i get homework..i dont feel liek doing it..like i get too lazy or just dont wanna at all...i guess its a habbit of mine..its bin like this since 5th grade..i tried manny times to keep on doing mi How and i do it for like 3 or 4 days then after that i'm like ..oh forget it...i donno what to do...

Shawn - **USA**

Answer
It is easy to put off the work, because it is difficult and not that much fun to do. The problem is that you get further behind and it almost makes school unpleasant.

High school can be a fun time, if you have things in control. With anything in life, you've got to take care of business before you can have fun. Also, it depends on what you see yourself doing after you get out of school.

One thing to do is to consider a few things you'd like and write them done. It may be getting your own car or some things like that. But also it should be the grades you'd like to get. Often get-

Doing Homework

ting the car depends on your grades. Write these goals down and put them where you can see them every day. That will give you some motivation.

Also, set aside a specific time only for homework. It takes some discipline, but don't do anything but homework during that time. If you don't feel like doing it, still stay at your desk and put in that time, even if just sit there and daydream. That should help you get going. Perhaps do the easiest stuff first, just to get some things completed.

I'm sure you will succeed, because you want to. It just takes a little self-discipline to become a champion.

Zipping is not always the best choice

Question
October 2

Time does matter. But "zipping" through homework as quick as you can is not always the right choice. Usually while other students try to finish their homework quickly they tend to overlook information, write down incorrect answers, and have poorer quality work than the students that take their time and try to learn something as they work. Time is not everything.

Lama - a high school sophomore - **USA**

Answer
You are absolutely right. If students carelessly rush through their homework, they can easily skip over material or not learn as well as they should. This was really aimed at those who easily get sidetracked or who spend too much time but achieve little.

The real goal in homework is learning and doing your best job.

I appreciate your comments. You sound like a real champion.

Feedback on Homework

Homework doesn't interest me

Question
March 8

I am having trouble with my homework. I can never get it done because it just does not interest me and I don't want to get bad grades. I have tried listening to music but that does not help....ahhh!! It's just really frustrating!!!! Can you help??? Please?? Thank you and write back ASAP I am a ninth grader love me!

KIMBERELY - **USA**

Answer
It is tough to do homework when the subject doesn't interest you. But since you don't want to get bad grades, you know you need to get it done. The big thing is not to waste too much time thinking how boring it is. Rather, since it is something you have to do—like chores around the house—do it right away and get it done, so you have time for other things. Many students put of the unpleasant, thus ending up spending more time that they need too.

Another thought is that if you are good in a subject, you usually become interested in it, because it is good to get the positive feedback and good grades.

Listening to music is OK if you are into your homework, but it doesn't help if you aren't. In that case, you just need to blast through it in a place where you can concentrate.

Being in the ninth grade, I'm sure there are many things to look forward to in the next several years. Start thinking in terms of having fun in high school, in learning a lot of stuff and not being bored.

Doing Homework

Best wishes in being able to get your homework done. I know you have it in you to be a champion in school and to get some real good grades.

Homework is too boring

Question
September 24

My problem is that homework is too boring so I go on an other planet. What can I do?

(no name given) - **USA**

Answer
It is tough if the homework is boring. But ask yourself: Why it is boring to me? Is it because you don't like the subject or you aren't interested in it? Or is it because it is too easy for you and just seems like "busy work"?

In either case, that is why I always felt it is good to try to zip through your homework. It is like doing chores at home. Chores are a pain and can be boring, and you probably avoid doing them. But if you have to do them, I hope you don't drag it out, so it takes you a lot of time.

Likewise with homework, try to blast through it, doing a good enough job to get a decent grade. It takes some discipline, though.

It is just something you have to go through. Hopefully, as you advance in school, you can take classes that are real interesting or a challenge to you—things where you will actually want to do the homework. That is something to look forward to.

Does homework in morning

Question
September 14

I have trouble doing homework at night. I can't do it in the evening either. Instead, I'll be ending up sleeping at night and I'll wake up at 3 or 4 in the morning just to get my homework done. And as a result, I've got dark rings under my eyes. I can't help it. Do you think I should carry on with the way I cope with my schoolwork?

Hafizah Abd Latif – **Saudi Arabia**

Answer
Some people are not effective at night and do their best work in the morning. There is nothing wrong with getting up extra early to do your homework, provided you go to bed early enough to get sufficient sleep. But that is sometimes difficult to do when there are other people up and around.

One advantage of getting up so early to do your homework is that you make sure you get it done without hesitation. Often at night a person takes much more time to do the homework because of distractions.

If you can, try to get some of your homework done in the afternoon. Then you won't have to do as much in the morning.

But also, it is still a good idea to try to do work at night. You may run into situations later on where you will need to do work at night.

I hope this helps. Let me know how things work out.

Doing Homework

Friend might copy

Question
September 5

I think I would study by my self cuz that person could copy your work and get you in trouble.

(no name given) - **USA**

Answer
If you study with another person, you must trust that person. Also, the idea is to be able to discuss things, but not to share the solutions to problems, like in math.

Some people do better when studying with another person, while some prefer to study alone. I always studied alone.

Homework is #1 priority

Question
August 6

I found your site and I think it is so wonderful for you to give out free information like that. You have no idea how much it helped me! Thank you so much. Also, do you have ways to make homework your #1 priority? I still need help with that. Thanks.

Alexandra - **USA**

Answer
I'm glad the material has been useful to you. Your homework shouldn't be your number 1 priority. Rather, #1 should be getting good grades and learning something. Homework is just a means to an end.

Feedback on Homework

If you can picture yourself gaining knowledge and getting good grades, you will find that you'll be more motivated to do your homework. But sometimes it can be a drag, especially if there is something else to do. In those cases, it is good to get it done right away, so you can then do other things.

Procrastinates

Question
April 14

My name is Katie, and I am a junior in high school. I have raw smarts and am capable of getting good grades, and I still do pretty well, but my focus wavers. I am already employing most of the suggestions you made, but when it comes time to work sometimes I just can't do it and end up having to wake myself up at four in the morning to finish it. I am getting really stressed out because I want to do well, but I just can't stay on task. I mean, even now I was supposed to be doing my Chem homework but instead ended up writing to you. Do you have any suggestions?

Katie - **USA**

Answer
Not being motivated on doing homework can be because you're not that interested in the material, it is hard work, or there is something more enjoyable to do. There probably are some other reasons a person would put off doing homework or other tasks.

Although it is tough to get motivated if you aren't that interested, the biggest motivation can be looking to the future. Next year is your last year in high school, and if you go on to college, you want to get good grades now to help you then.

One thing you can try to get yourself to focus on completing a homework assignment is to get yourself pumped up and then blitz through the assignment. Walk around your room, like you

Doing Homework

are ready to start a fight or to take on a tough challenge. Take some deep breaths. Then BOOM! Sit down and blast through that assignment.

Then give yourself a reward, when you finish it.

If you have a lot to do, I guess it is best to do the most unpleasant assignment first, to get it out of the way. If it is a real long assignment, break it up by changing subject every 45 minutes.

I hope these ideas help. Visualize straight A's for Katie.

Section 4: Taking Tests

Your grades depend on your test scores. You can display your knowledge in class and in your homework, but unless you can verify that knowledge in a test, you will not get a good grade. Thus, you really need to learn to be good at taking tests. It is a special skill that separates the students with the top grades from those who barely get by.

Often students worry so much about tests that they get anxious and actually go blank during an exam. Improving your skills in taking tests will help to prevent such a disaster from happening.

Chapters in this section:

1. Be Good at Taking Tests
2. Practice Taking Tests
3. Preparation Needed to Excel in Tests
4. Mental Process in Preparing for a Test
5. Avoiding Goofing Up Tests
6. Feedback on Tests

Taking Tests

Be Good at Taking Tests

Besides understanding and remembering the important parts of the subject matter, you need to be good at taking tests in order to receive good grades in school. Being able to do well in tests is a special skill, distinct from simply being smart or knowing the subject matter.

A major part of your grade is determined from your test scores. Problems that students have include improper preparation, test anxiety and working too slow. You can become good at taking tests by thoroughly preparing for the test and by actually practicing test-taking.

Importance of test-taking skill

A major part of your grade is determined from your test scores. Some teachers give their students numerous quizzes and tests, while others base most of the grade on a final exam.

You could be the smartest student in your class—leading discussions and doing well on your homework—but if you have problems taking tests, you simply will not get the grade you probably deserve.

Problems students have

Many students have problems concerning taking tests.

Poor preparation
Part of the skill in taking a test is in the preparation for the test. Trying to study all of the material covered is a poor way to prepare. It is called "cramming" for the test. There are also some students who aren't sure what is important and what may be on the test.

Taking Tests

Of course, there are students who don't even bother to study for a test. That is just plain foolish.

Work too slow
Some students work on a test at a pace that is too slow to allow them to finish the test in time. They spend too much time on unimportant parts of the exam and take too much time in making a decision on an answer.

When the test time is almost up, they then rush, which can result in hasty or incorrect answers.

Test anxiety
Other students get so nervous before and during a test such that their minds seem to go blank and they can't remember what they had learned.

Improving test-taking skills
You should be well-prepared for taking a test or exam. Practicing taking tests is a good method to make yourself ready.

Prepare for test
Since the test is a special situation, you should prepare well ahead of time.

Instead of trying to study all of the material covered before the test, you should know specifically what to study. Taking notes in class and highlighting important parts of your textbook are useful methods. Also, look for clues from your teach about what is important and may be in the test.

Taking a test or exam is similar to what an athlete would do before a big game or a professional musician would do before a performance or show.

You must prepare yourself mentally or psychologically, such that you are confident and ready to perform. You obviously must prepare yourself with knowledge of the subject, such that you understand the material and remember the facts. Finally, you should be physically and mentally prepared, so that you will be alert and at your best when taking the test.

Practice taking tests
When you take a test in school, you are usually working under the pressure of finishing the test in within a certain time limit. Also, you usually cannot look in your textbook or notes for information or an answer.

Since this can be a pressure-packed situation, it is a good idea to practice taking tests or to practice working under such conditions, so that you become adept at it. One method is to practice doing homework exercises as if it was a test, setting a time limit for doing the homework exercises and not using notes or your textbook to help you with the answers.

Summary
Since your grades depend on your scores in tests and exams, being good at test-taking is important. Improper preparation, test anxiety and working too slow are reasons some students do poorly in tests. You can become good at taking tests by thoroughly preparing for the test and by actually practicing test-taking.

Practice Taking Tests

If you want to be good at playing a musical instrument, you must practice playing it. The same holds true for being able to do well in tests.

Practicing taking tests will improve your ability to work under the pressure of answering questions without your book and under strict time constraints. Sometimes doing homework as if it was a test, competing with friends, or taking sample tests are ways to practice.

Why practice?
One big difference between taking a test and doing homework is that you are working under the pressure of finishing the test in within a certain time limit. The other difference is that you usually cannot look in your textbook or notes for information or an answer.

Since the whole idea is to be good at taking tests, the more you practice taking tests, the better you get doing them. You can practice by making believe your homework is a test, or you can take tests in study aids.

There are also some students that know the material but freeze up when working under pressure, so they often don't do well in tests. These methods will also help them gain the confidence they need.

Practice with homework
You might try practicing doing homework exercises, as if it was a test. In other words, set a time limit for doing certain homework exercises—perhaps using an alarm clock to provide some

pressure—and you don't use notes or your textbook to help you. When time is up, you can give yourself a grade and go back and finish the problems you couldn't do.

This also could be a good way to learn more and get through your homework more rapidly. If you have to solve a number of math problems, or you have to write an essay, doing it under time constraints will help you "zip through your homework."

Obviously, there are many homework assignments where this may not work. In some cases, you really need to refer to the book or your notes to get your homework done.

Other ways to practice
There are some other ways to practice taking tests.

Competing
Competing with a friend to see who finishes the homework first can be a way to practice performing under pressure. Obviously, you have to get the answers right or do a good job in the homework, besides being able to finish first.

Also, remember to follow the *School for Champions* philosophy of congratulating the winner—whether it is yourself or the other person. The idea isn't to win, rather to improve the skills of both of you.

Taking sample tests
For students trying to get into college, there are books that help you prepare for the SAT and similar exams. They have sample tests to take as practice. This is another possibility to hone your test–taking skill.

Summary
Being good at tests is important in getting good grades. You can improve your test-taking abilities by practicing taking tests when doing your homework, competing with friends or using practice tests.

Preparation Needed to Excel in Tests

Preparing for a test is almost as important as actually taking the test. You need to prepare mentally or psychologically, You need to prepare with knowledge of the subject. And finally, you must be in good physical condition to take the test.

Preparation in these three areas will give you an edge in achieving excellence.

Preparing mentally or psychologically

You must be mentally or psychologically prepared for a test, just like an athletic team must be mentally prepared for a big game.

Factors involved

There are several steps to take to mentally prepare for a test:

1. The first step is to be motivated by the importance of test to you.

2. Then set a goal of the type of grade you want to get.

3. Next, be aware of the difficulty of test and the challenge it will present.

4. Finally, be confident and sure of your knowledge of the subject matter and in your ability to perform in a test.

Then you are ready to do your best.

Taking Tests

Learn from championship teams
The lesson from championship teams is that they never take a game or an opponent for granted. They realize the importance of each game and prepare the same way, whether the opponent is strong or weak. They have a goal of doing their best at all times and reaping the rewards from winning.

Don't get overconfident
Some students get overconfident and don't prepare properly for the test. These students should check *Avoid Goofing Up Tests* for ways to rectify that situation.

Preparing your knowledge
Obviously, you should have learned the material well before the test. The preparations you make concerning your knowledge relates to reviewing the material. Different types of classes require different types of study.

Study of facts
If a test is concerned with how well you remember facts, don't study for it be trying to memorize everything. Rather, learn concepts and memorize key words.

Cramming
I have a friend who would always cram for his exams. He never seemed to study until just before a test when he would stay up all night. He received good grades because of his excellent short-term memory. However, I think he forgot much of what he had learned afterwards.

This method may work for some students, but I don't recommend it myself.

Problem solving study
For tests in the sciences, doing a good job on your homework is usually the best way to prepare, since these tests often concern problem solving. Memorization for science tests doesn't work as well. Understanding is more important.

Preparing physically

Your physical condition affects your mental abilities. You should watch what you eat and drink before taking a test and get plenty of rest. Also, being in good physical shape allows for more blood to get to your brain.

Watch sugar and food

You usually want to be alert before a test. It is not a good idea to have sugary drinks or a heavy meal before a test. This is because you can get sleepy. Much of your blood goes to your stomach instead of your brain, where you really need the oxygen for thinking.

Get sleep

Some students seem to be able to do well on a test after staying up all night, but most need a good night's sleep to be at their best. In general, if you are tired, you are not as effective as if you are well rested.

Get regular exercise

A person who gets regular physical exercise has a body and mind that uses its oxygen more effectively than someone completely out of shape. Even exercising a few days before a test can make a noticeable difference on your thinking powers.

Say no to drinks

For college students old enough to drink, alcohol before a test is not a good idea. You should not have such drinks for at least three days before a test or your mind may be like mush.

Summary

Being good at tests is important. You can improve your test-taking abilities by knowing how to prepare for a test. This means to get yourself up psychologically and ready to perform at your best. Of course, you must study and know the material upon which you will be tested. Finally, you should be well rested and mentally alert for the test.

Mental Process in Preparing for a Test

Most people go through a similar mental process in preparing to take a test.

Before you start to study for a test, you usually perform a subconscious evaluation of your motivation and expectations. This often determines how hard and how well you will study. Preparation of the test then consists of refreshing your memory of material learned and then getting mentally or emotionally prepared to take the test. For your own enlightenment, it is good to know this process.

Mental process

It is useful to take a look at the mental process involved in preparing for a test.

1. When a test is coming up, you subconsciously evaluate:

    a. How important getting a good grade is to you

    b. How well you know the subject matter and how well you can do in tests

    c. How difficult you expect the test to be and what material the teacher will most likely cover in the test

2. Then they prepare for the test:

    a. Refresh your memory by studying

    b. Refresh your body and brain for alertness, endurance and such

c. Establish the proper mental state, such as being psyched up and ready to perform

3. Finally, you take the test, executing your preparations

Subconscious evaluations

When you realize that a test is coming up and you have to study for it, you subconsciously go through some evaluations that will determine your motivation for that studying.

Importance of grade

You consider how important getting a good grade is, as opposed to the work required to study. Some students just don't care if they get a good grade or not. Others are trying to upset their parents or the teacher by actually wanting to get a bad grade.

If getting a good grade is important, you are motivated to study.

Knowledge level

You consider how well you know the subject and how well you usually do in tests.

If you are confident of your abilities, you will tend to study more. If you are not confident, you may be anxious and not study effectively or you may simply give up. On the other hand, if you are overconfident, you also may not bother to study, because you feel you can fake your way through the test.

Have sufficient knowledge and confidence that you don't go to one extreme or the other.

Difficulty of material

A third evaluation you usually make is how difficult you expect the test to be. This is a combination of the subject matter and your knowledge of the type of tests the teacher gives.

Mental Process in Preparing for a Test

Combining your motivation of getting a good grade, your knowledge level and the expected difficulty of the test provides a good criteria for the level of studying you need to do.

Preparing for test

In preparing for a test, you refresh your memory by studying, refresh your body and brain for alertness and endurance and establish the proper mental state for taking the test.

Refresh memory

Studying for a test is simply refreshing your memory by reviewing the material. This is not the time to start going over new material or trying to solve problems that should have been previously done.

A good way to refresh your memory is to write down key words that will spark your recollection.

Refresh body and mind

Since a test is so important to your grade, you should be prepared with an alert brain and body. Party time is after the test, not before. Get some light exercise and a good night's sleep before the test.

Sometimes getting rest the night before is difficult if you have to cram for the test. But if you prepare properly, you should not have to spend the whole night studying.

Refresh mental state

Come into the test with confidence and a positive attitude. Know the material and be in a mental state of being ready to get that "A" on this test.

Summary

Before you study for a test, you usually go through subconscious evaluations that determine your motivation and amount of studying needed. Then, when you do study for the test, it should simply be a form of refreshing your memory and mental state. Also refresh your body and brain before the test.

Avoiding Goofing Up Tests

Have you ever taken a test that you thought you could easily passed, only to make some silly or bonehead mistakes that really hurt your grade? More than a few students have done that. And some seem to do it over and over again.

There are reasons students goof up tests, from being overconfident to having poor attitudes. Preparation is important in avoiding the problem. Interestingly enough, this is very similar to what happens to some athletic teams. The solution to that problem is not that difficult. You just need to have the right attitude and be better mentally prepared.

Reasons some students goof

There are several problem areas that can cause students to goof up or do poorly on a test that they could have passed. Students can be overconfident, they can underestimate the potential difficulty of the test, or they can feel that passing the test is not important to them.

Some are overconfident

Some students can get overconfident in their knowledge of the subject matter. They think they know the material better than they actually do. It is easy for students to misjudge their own knowledge, and when they realize what they don't know, it is too late.

What happens more often, though, is that some feel they are smart enough to be able to guess their way through a test. So they don't bother studying the material. They are overconfident in their ability to figure things out.

In either case, overconfidence can result in lower grades on tests. Does this apply to you?

Taking Tests

Some underestimate difficulty
Another thing that can happen is that students underestimate the difficulty of the test. They expect an easy test, but the teacher throws in a real tough one that they hadn't prepared for.

Another facet of this is if the teacher covers material in the test that they weren't expecting. That can happen, especially if you weren't paying attention in class.

Some feel test not important
Finally, there are students who don't feel that getting a good grade is important to them, so they don't bother studying or even trying. Such students may be trying to punish their parents, have a poor image of themselves, or are just plain foolish. Hopefully, you are not one of these students.

Results of negative attitudes
What usually happens when students have any of these unfortunate attitudes is that they do not properly prepare for the test:

1. They don't review or study for the test

2. They get involved in activities before the test that result in being tired and not mentally alert

3. They are not in the proper state or psyched-up for the test

Any of these situations can result in failure.

Similar to some athletic teams
The whole scenario of making unnecessary mistakes in a test is often seen in athletic teams who are playing an opponent that is not considered as good as them. You may have seen this with your school team or favorite professional team. What happens is that they don't get ready for the game, and the other team simply tries harder.

They don't get ready
The team thinks the game will be easy, so they don't prepare themselves physically, they don't study the game plan, and they don't mentally or psychologically get themselves ready to play as much as they usually do. When the game starts, they are sluggish and make foolish mistakes. They don't play up to their ability.

Other team tries harder
Meanwhile, the other team—which was supposed to be easily beaten—makes thorough preparations and play at their best, thus winning the game.

Preparation is key
What you can learn by looking at students or athletic teams that have the ability to excel, but yet who come up short when it really counts, is that they often don't prepare properly.

Championship teams prepare
The lesson from championship teams is that they never take a game or an opponent for granted. They realize the importance of each game and prepare the same way, whether the opponent is strong or weak. They have a goal of doing their best at all times and reaping the rewards from winning.

These are the same attitudes you should have toward taking a test. To avoid goofing up test, you have to take them more seriously.

Steps to take to excel
Steps to take to do well in a test are:

1. Set a goal to do your best in every test, perhaps even aiming at getting a 100 or A for a grade.

2. Prepare your mind, body, and attitude for excelling in the test. Try to be consistent in your preparations, not doing more or less than is necessary.

Taking Tests

3. Go and give it your best shot. Then celebrate your success and learn from your mistakes.

Follow these steps to do well in your tests and to avoid making unnecessary mistakes.

Summary

Some students good up tests because they are overconfident, underestimate difficulty, or just don't care. The same has been seen on occasion with sports teams. The attitude of sufficient preparation and then giving it your best is the way to avoid goofing up tests.

Feedback on Tests

Students from around the world send email to the *School for Champions* with questions and comments on various aspects of getting good grades in school. The following letters concern problems in taking tests. Note that the letters have not been edited for correct grammar or spelling.

Stressed out because I can't remember

Question
October 4

Studying is one of the hardest aspects of school for me. I can never remember anything i have learned from class after a few days even if I review it the night after class. Because of that, I have to review everything in detail all over again. For me, this takes at least 6-7 hours until i am completely satisfied with what I have learned. Is there any other way for me to acquire information faster? Please help me! I have a test in two days that I have to study for and I am stressed out!!!

Rachel - **Canada**

Answer
One thing to try is to take notes in class. You can put down what you think are important points the teacher makes. Likewise, when you study, try to either write down important points or mark or highlight them in the book. You don't want to write down or mark everything, but only enough so that it will give you a clue when you study later. Often just seeing a few words will help remind you of what you had read.

Taking Tests

Another thing is to observe how you are studying. Do you picture things or do you like to hear the sounds of words? Some students are more effective picturing things and even sentences, while other are better in hearing them. Those students often talk to themselves while studying.

The biggest thing in every class is to learn the concept. Even in a class like history, if you catch on to the concept of what was being taught, you are better able to recreate things in you mind, making it easier to study.

Also, don't seek perfection. You need to have enough confidence in your abilities to do just enough to get a good grade, but not so much that you are worn out.

I hope these ideas help and that you will do well in all your tests.

Just got an F in Social Studies

Question
September 27

I had a great time reading the helpful hints. I just got an F on a Social Studies test, it was on facts and location of things like the Mississippi R.I studied, but i still got an F, any advices? And give me a list of times to do homework and when to play, like 9:00am to 9:30am, read book.

Tommy - **USA**

Answer
In a course like Social Studies, it is good to get an idea of what the teacher thinks are important facts. But also, you need to pay attention to things like the pictures in the books. They are good to visualize later and help remember various facts.

Feedback on Tests

Ask your Social Studies teacher if he or she can give you some pointers so that you won't fail the next test. Teachers don't want their students to fail, since it makes them look bad. Usually, they will be glad to help with some tips.

You need to pick times to study that will fit into your schedule and still allow time to play or watch TV. If you have time in the morning, you can study then, but you need to be careful not to leave too much to do in the morning. You don't want to be rushed. That is why most finish their work in the evening. Then if a little extra needs to be done, they can finish in the morning.

Best wishes in your classes. The fact that you are trying to improve means that you must have what it takes to advance and improve. Pick a good grade you want in your class and then shoot for that grade.

Goes blank during tests

Question
March 23

My name is Chiedum, I a junior in Berkley high school in Michigan. I am a very hardworking student. I pay attention in class but when it comes to test I totally blank out, I get really nervous (especially in chemistry and math) I notice that during the first day of school when school starts I do really good but second semester I start becoming physically tired (during the snow). if you have any advice for me on how to boost up my study skills. I would like it. It wasn't always like this. In elementary school I get the highest grade in all my classes good or bad teachers. But now I am not doing as well as I want. Is it because I am pushing my self to hard?

Thanks for you time

Chiedum - **USA**

Taking Tests

Answer

One thing you can do is to practice taking tests. Put yourself under the pressure of time constraints and not being able to look up things in your book. You can try this when you are doing your homework or have someone make up a test for you. This will get you "in condition" for taking the test, just like an athlete does before a game.

In this way, you should not be getting as nervous before the test.

Math is a subject where you need skill in solving problems. There is not much memory work there. When you take the test, you must become very methodical. Some people talk to themselves when doing math problems at home. If you do that, then do it during the test too (but not aloud).

Chemistry is both concept and memory. It is worth skimming through your notes just before the test. Again, it is worth being very methodical when you go through the problems. This will also reduce nervousness from trying to go too fast.

Some people get down during the gloomy winter. You might try to use a sunlight light bulb in your study area. They cost a couple dollars more, but the light is more like sunlight and helps people feel better in the winter.

Mix up your homework and try to take time for fun. If you work too hard or try too hard, your mind can get dull.

Best wishes in school, and I am sure you will become a champion.

Studies hard but freezes up in tests

Question
January 29

Hello, my name is April

I'd like to thank you for all the helpful information that you put on this website, but I need some more help in school. I work really hard and I study really hard. The subjects that I need help in are math, grammar, and French.

Even though I study, I'm still not doing well in those subjects. I freeze on tests. The material that I study seems so different than what it is on the test.

I'm not getting much encouragement either. So, I was wondering if you could give me some advice, if it's not too much trouble.

April - **USA**

Answer
One of the tricks in doing well in tests is to know what material to study. Often the teacher will give some indication what is important. You have to keep your eyes open for those clues. Sometimes it is good to ask your friends in class what they think is going to be covered in the test. Discussing it might give you ideas.

In many classes like math and grammar, it is not obvious what the point of it is. You can sometimes get a better idea from looking at lower level books. Like, you could go to the library and look at some simple books on the type of math you are studying. You just skim through to try to get a better idea about it.

Taking Tests

With French, you not only have to memorize the words, but you also need to learn their grammar and pronunciation. Using flash card can help sometimes. Also practicing with a friend from your class can help learn quicker.

The thing is to not try to study harder but to study smarter. And you've got to make sure you are studying the right stuff.

As far as freezing up on tests goes, it means you are either not confident in your knowledge or in your ability to take tests. I think part of it has to do with being sure of what material to study for the test.

Although it is tough to do, it might be good to talk to your teachers and ask what you can do to get better grades in their classes. You might get some good suggestions. If nothing else, the teacher will know you are concerned. Also, you can tell that you're often not sure of what material will be covered in the test. The teacher may then try to make it clearer in class.

It would be nice if someone gave you encouragement, because it seems to make things easier. But if your teachers or others around you don't give encouragement, you just have to depend on yourself. Give yourself a pat on the back every time you finish an assignment. Say to yourself, "Good work, April." That helps you build up your own confidence and esteem. If you goof up, tell yourself, "I'll do better next time."

I hope these ideas will help. Since you are trying to improve, you certainly have what it takes to be a champion in what you try.

Best wishes in getting good grades in your classes. And let me know how things turn out.

Feedback on Tests

I still do bad on tests

Question
March 19

No matter how many times I study, i still do bad on the tests. I'm smart enough to get all A's in school but people say I'm not trying hard enough. i was on the a honor roll once. What do I do?

Kaoru - **USA**

Answer
If you've been on the honor roll before, you know you can do it again. Think back of what you were doing then.

If you don't do well in test, you may not be studying the right things. You have to make sure you understand what is important to the teacher, because that is the material that probably will be on the tests. Be observant to get an idea of what is important.

The big thing in studying is to study smart. Be efficient and effective in your studying. You also need to know yourself and your style of learning.

Practicing taking test by doing your homework within a time limit to put extra pressure can often help those who freeze up during a test.

Write down the grades you want to get on a piece of paper and pin it on the wall in your study area. That will help keep you focused.

I hope these ideas help and that you get all A's.

Section 5: Teachers

Teachers can be a blessing or a curse. Sometimes you can get a teacher who will provide knowledge in an interesting manner, such that you enjoy going to class. But other times you may get a teacher who is a complete jerk and acts so mean to everyone. Also, there are some teachers who don't know the subject matter very well.

You can see it is important to try to get good teachers and to know how to deal with those that may give you problems.

1. When the Teacher is a Jerk
2. Getting a Good Teacher
3. Feedback on Teachers

Teachers

When the Teacher is a Jerk

Sometimes you can get a teacher who is unpleasant, real mean or just a complete jerk. It makes you wonder why some teachers act that way.

Ideally, you would like to avoid having such a teacher, but often you don't have a choice. It may be too late to change, and you are stuck with the person for the rest of the semester. In such a situation, you have a choice of either giving the teacher a rough time or trying to cope with the situation. Since the teacher has power over whether you pass or fail, it is in your interest to try a positive strategy.

Why they act that way

You might wonder why your teacher acts so mean or unpleasant. There may be numerous reasons for this behavior. The teacher may hate his or her job and thus takes it out on the students. The teacher may have an unpleasant way of trying to motivate the students. There may be a personality conflict between you and the teacher. Or perhaps the teacher is just plain mean.

Hates job
Some teachers love children and love what they do. But there are a few teachers—for one reason or another—who simply hate what they are doing. They act grumpy in class and can be unpleasant. Some may even take it out their anger on students.

May have wrong way of motivating
The correct way to motivate someone is by giving encouragement and praise. Unfortunately, some teachers think they can motivate their students by yelling at them or by acting tough.

It is unpleasant, but you must realize that most teachers want their students to do well, but some just express themselves in a negative manner that can turn students off to them.

May be a personality conflict
Some people just don't get along. Their personalities are completely opposite, such that they grate on each other.

You may look at your teacher as a complete jerk because of the way he or she acts or appears. There is something about the person that you don't like, and it is reflected in the way you act toward the person. The teacher may feel your attitude and reciprocate with negative feelings towards you.

But it is also possible that your personality is such that it gets on the teacher's nerves. You may talk too much in class or have an "attitude" that the teacher doesn't like. If you run into a number of teachers who don't seem to like you, it might be a good idea to take a close look at how you act. You may be the jerk.

Giving a rough time
Some students will give a rough time to teacher they don't like. They will act rude or cause trouble in class just to give the teacher problems. Perhaps the student will refuse to do homework or cut class just to avoid the teacher or to get the teacher angry.

Not a good idea
Is giving a teacher a rough time in class a good approach for solving the problem of a teacher you don't like or one who doesn't act nice?

If your goal is to get through school with reasonable grades and with the minimum of hassles, giving a teacher a rough time is not the best route to take.

Remember that the teacher has power over what grade you get. Giving the teacher a rough time because you think he or she is a jerk can be suicide for your grades. It isn't worth getting poor grades for the sake of showing someone up—unless you are a glutton for punishment.

It is better to use a positive strategy to handle a problem teacher.

When the Teacher is a Jerk

Making the best of the situation

If you get a class where you don't like the teacher or don't get along with him or her, you need to develop a strategy to handle the situation in the best way possible for your well-being. One idea is to try to get on the good side of the teacher. You can also keep a low profile and just cope in this class.

Be on the good side

It is always worthwhile to be on the good side of the teacher, even if you don't like him or her. Simply being cordial and making the best of the situation will make your time with the teacher less unpleasant. In fact, you may be surprised to find out that the teacher isn't all that bad.

Keeping a low profile

Sometimes trying to get on the good side of a teacher who has an attitude toward you can backfire.

> When I was a senior in high school, I took a class in Physics. In the first semester, my grade was an A. But then in the second semester, with the same teacher, I somehow got on the bad side of him. Maybe I talked out of turn in class or something.
>
> So, I thought I would do an extra credit experiment in order to get back on the good side of him. Obviously, I wanted to get the best grade I could in this class. After school, I set up an electricity experiment, but then I accidentally touched two wires together and BOOM! There was a big flash. I shorted the wires, which blew out the fuses in the school!
>
> The Physics teacher's face got real red, his eyes bugged out, and a vein on his forehead showed. He was extremely angry with me. My effort to get on the good side of him had backfired.

Teachers

For the rest of the semester, I kept a low profile. I tried to be invisible in class, so I wouldn't give him a reason to give me any trouble. Although I deserved another A in the class, the teacher gave me a C. I could have contested the grade, but I was just glad to get out of that class.

The lesson it taught me was that no matter how hard you try, sometimes you just can't please certain small-minded people. I also learned to take the setback and move on with my life.

Can cope
If you have a jerk for a teacher, it is probably the best to simply try to cope with the situation to last out the semester. Perhaps in the next term you will get a better teacher.

Summary
Teachers who are unpleasant, real mean or just a complete jerks may act that way because they hate their jobs, have a poor way of motivating students or just don't like you. It is not a good idea to give such a teacher a rough time, because the teacher has the power to give you a poor grade and to make your life miserable in the process.

Getting a Good Teacher

In college and in most high schools, students select the courses and schedule they want. What is also important is to select the best teacher for the course. Many students don't think about selecting a teacher, but the extra research involved can be well worth the effort and result in better grades and fewer headaches.

How to find out about teachers
Learning about the quality of potential teachers takes some work and research.

Check rating sheets
Some high schools and colleges allow the students to complete evaluation sheets on teacher or instructors. Why this is not done as a regular practice, I don't know. Students or parents are paying for the education, so students should get the best teachers possible.

In schools with teacher evaluations, students can see the evaluation of potential instructors. Evaluations help students make the decision to include certain teachers in students' schedules. Surprisingly, many students do not bother to check these evaluations.

In many colleges where such an instructor evaluation system is not done, student entrepreneurs create and surveys and sell the results off campus. Fraternities and sororities often have such evaluations for their members.

Ask around
A very common way to find out about potential teachers is done by asking around. An older brother or sister or an acquaintance who has taken the course of interest can give his or her opinion

Teachers

on the teacher. Often information about good and bad teachers is disseminated through "the grapevine" and can be learned by asking around.

A good teacher
What makes a good teacher?

How does teacher grade?
The first thing students want to know is how the teacher grades. Certainly everyone wants a teacher who gives good grades.

> I was fortunate for 3 of the 4 years in high school to have an English teacher who gave out A's and B's to her students. I didn't select her, but I was just lucky to get her. She was also a good teacher and made the classes enjoyable.

The worst teachers are those who grade on a curve for the class, no matter how well the students do. In other words, if you did work that would have given you a B in a most classes, but you were in a class that consisting of geniuses, you might get a D in that class.

Having a teacher who grading on a curve like that can be discouraging and ruin your grade-point average.

How much homework is required?
Some teachers have a reputation for giving an excess amount of homework. You wonder if such a teacher realizes you have homework for other classes too.

What is really bad is if the homework is meaningless busy work.

On the other hand, if a teacher gives little or no homework, students are short-changed. If no studying is required, students feel that the class is meaningless. The problem with a class with too little homework is that you may have problems in future classes because of what you didn't learn.

Beware of teachers known for giving too much or too little homework. You want an education and need to think about having sufficient knowledge for future classes.

Is it interesting instruction?
The most important thing is whether or not the teacher provides instruction in a clear and interesting manner, such that the students will enjoy the class and really learn something. You can tell this when former students say, "That was a good class" or "She was a good teacher."

A major problem in colleges is that instructors aren't hired for their teaching skills. Instead instructors are hired for their ability to do research and write papers that bring in funding to the school. Also, some college instructors are from other areas or countries have accents that are extremely difficult to understand. The fact that colleges and universities many times disregard the quality of the instruction is a crime.

However, there are good teachers in all schools. You just need to look for them.

Course of action
If you are in a situation where you area able to select your instructors, it is worth your while to do some research about possible instructors.

An incoming freshman may have little choice in selecting instructors. But after that, you can start planning for the next 3 ½ years by checking around for resources and getting to know people in the school who have taken similar courses or subjects.

This type of research can help you get a better education, better grades and make your life in school more enjoyable.

Summary
It is worthwhile to find out who are the good teachers in your school and then try to enroll in classes taught by those good instructors. Some schools have formal or informal rating available to students. In other cases, you might need to ask people you know what they have heard about certain teachers. Grades, homework and quality instruction are important for your education.

Feedback on Teachers

Students from around the world send email to the *School for Champions* with questions and comments on various aspects of getting good grades in school. The following letters concern problems with teachers. Note that the letters have not been edited for correct grammar or spelling.

Why don't some teachers allow gum?

Question
October 14

When taking tests, why is it that some teachers allow gum and others don't? I just think it sucks.

Daneisha - **USA**

Answer
I never could understand why teachers care if a student chews gum or not. I think one problem is that many kids stick the gum under the desk when they are through with it. That can make a mess on the next person's clothes.

But if a student needs gum to relax when taking a test, it might not be a bad idea to let her chew the gum. Maybe the grades would be better.

Teachers

My Spanish teacher is grading unfairly

Question
November 15

My Spanish teacher is grading unfairly. She gives you extra credit and acts like its a grade. I did all my homework got A+ on every test except I didn't do extra credit. Guess what I got on my report card a 60!! Plus I got 100s 2 quarters back! How is that possible in 4 weeks!

Well I don't know what to do so please help.

Billy - **USA**

Answer
That doesn't sound right. Extra credit is supposed to be optional. It looks like what she calls extra credit is required work.

One thing you might think about is if there is any reason that she has something against you. Hopefully, you didn't complain about her to some friends, because it might have gotten back to her. Although it is not right for a teacher to lower grades for such a reason, it still happens.

The big thing is that you want to make sure you get the grades you deserve in that class. It would be a good idea to ask the teacher why you only got a 60, when you had done so well in the tests. Make sure you do not try to argue, but act like you simply want to know the reason. If she says you didn't do the extra credit, see if you can make it up to get your grade up higher.

Whatever the reason she gives, just remember that your goal is to get a decent grade, no matter how unfair she is. It isn't pleasant, but sometimes you have to jump through hoops to get by.

Certainly, try not to get this teacher again.

Feedback on Teachers

I hope these ideas help and that you will be able to start getting good grades in this class.

Teacher always nags and calls us fools

Question
November 11

My chemistry teacher is so proud of herself. Our school's the best one but she always nags that you are fool. She teaches us in a bad way for example in the questions about yields she answered us and when we said it's wrong, she said no. Then after one important test exam she said about the true way and said: "I wanted to examine you."

Now please tell me what shall I do and let me know if you know any chemistry teacher who can teach me online for high school, the last year. Thanks.

Sarah - **USA**

Answer
Your teacher mistakenly thinks that she can make her students better by belittling them. That is not a good way to teach, and it makes learning uncomfortable for the students. She may also have personality problems such that she is trying to prove she is much smarter than the students.

Although it may not be pleasant to have such a teacher, you will have to cope with her for the rest of the semester. Your big goal is to get a good grade, so you will need to try to figure out what she wants plus do some extra studying on the side. You can use our Chemistry lessons, although they are pretty basic.

If you are having trouble in the class, you might try to get a tutor. Unfortunately, that can be expensive. Another thing is to perhaps try studying or discussing homework with some friends in class.

Teachers

I hope these ideas help and that you will be able to get through this class with good grades.

Teacher gave me a lunch detention

Question
October 29

My teacher is mean. She gave me lunch detention because I didn't turn in my book report!!!

(no name given) - **USA**

Answer
Sorry to hear you got a detention. I don't think it is right for a teacher to do that for not turning in a book report. The fair way would be to give a zero grade for the report.

My teacher is picking on me

Question
October 12

Hello, my teacher is picking on me. If someone is talking to me I'm the one who always gets in trouble. I am afraid to ask him a question about my work because I'm sick of him always putting me down and he also tries to embarrass me in front of the class. he says to me if you don't want to be in my class, then just leave. I might just do that next time he says that.

(no name given) - **Australia**

Answer
It is unfortunate that some teachers behave so poorly. There is no reason for a teacher to put down a student or embarrass the student. Those are just poor teaching methods.

Feedback on Teachers

The big thing is that you want to make it through the class with a minimum of hassle and also get a decent grade. The first thing to do is to completely avoid talking about him to your friends or other students. Often word can get back to the teacher and cause resentment. Another thing is to try to keep a low profile in class to prevent him from having an excuse to pick on you.

Also, keep track of the times you feel he is unfairly picking on your or embarrassing you. You might write down the information. If things get too bad, you might show your parents and then have them complain to the school principal. But complaining should be a last resort because sometimes the principal will side with the teacher, resulting in more problems for you.

Just try to make it through the class and make sure you don't get this guy as a teacher the next time around.

Best wishes, and I hope things work out for you.

Chemistry teacher picks on me

Question
September 21

What should I do my chemistry teacher does not like me because I am the only one in my class of all girls who is not skinny and dressed in skirts and make up. He only called on my all day no one else in a row he called on one other person after he called on me 2 in a row. I have a c in his class and a lot of the girls in my class are failing but he won't ask them. He even gives them answers on the test if they could flirt enough. This is low and I don't want to deal with this I ended up leaving 10 minutes before class was over because I was in tears.

It was embarrassing to only be the one he wants to answer a question

Kim – **USA**

Teachers

Answer

It certainly is not pleasant being in a class where it seems that the teacher does not like you and is picking on you. The big problem is that you are stuck in his class for the rest of the semester. Also, it is really difficult to prove to anyone that he is picking on you.

Your goal in this class is to get a passing grade and make it through the semester or term without too much hassle. One thing is not to worry or think about any of the other girls flirting with him or getting special attention. That can just get you more upset and sends out negative "vibrations" that the teacher can pick up. Just try to ignore that stuff and think of what is best for you.

Also, don't think that the thin girls who dress up and have make up are any better or more appealing than you. If you take care of yourself, aren't sloppy or such, then you can appear just as good as them. But if you don't take care of your appearance, you should start. It shows you have respect for yourself.

If your teacher calls on you, one way to look at it is: "I guess he doesn't think anyone else knows this answer, so that is why he is calling on me." What I'm getting at is not to act like it is a punishment. If it looks like you're happy to answer him (even if you don't know the answer), perhaps that will discourage him from bugging you.

The long and the short of it is to be brave and think well of yourself. Try to get through this class without letting your teacher make you feel bad. You might even prove yourself a champion in the class.

I hope these ideas help. Best wishes, and I am sure things will get better for you in your chemistry class.

Feedback on Teachers

Teacher is sexually harassing

Question
September 18

Hello, well I was just wondering what happened when a teacher tries to sexually harass a student? Should I report it, talk to my mum or talk to him? Please help me I'm not sure what to do!

(no name given) - **Australia**

Answer
If you think a teacher is truly sexually harassing a student, you need to take action to prevent it from happening again. Sometimes it may be innocent kidding by the teacher, but he should know better than that. But other times a teacher may actually "make a play" for a student. That is very bad.

You could talk to the teacher and tell him that you don't like his actions. Hopefully, that would cause him to stop. If it doesn't, you could report him to your mum and/or report him.

But it is not often easy to talk to the teacher like that. If that is the case, it might be good to discuss it with your mother.

The thing is that if he was just kidding, you want him to simply stop. But if he is nasty, then he should be reported. You need to decide which it is and what action to take.

I hope this gives you some ideas of how to handle this difficult situation.

Teachers

How can I be liked by the teacher?

Question
August 4

How can I be liked by the teacher without being the teacher's pet and with the other kids liking me?

(no name given) - **USA**

Answer
Teachers seem to like students that are really trying over those that are just getting by or don't care. Also, if the teacher gets to know the student, he or she will like the student more. But also, teachers obviously don't like students how make trouble in class or who bad-mouth the teacher outside of class.

One thing you can try is to see the teacher after class some time and ask the teacher for some tips on how you can do better in the class. Perhaps tell of your plans to go to college or get a job or such. This will show your interest and will usually get you on the good side of the teacher.

Also, if you see the teacher in the hall, give a greeting.

Neither of these things will peg you as "teacher's pet" and get others to dislike you.

But note too that in some rare cases there may be a personality conflict with a teacher. If you sense that, the best bet is to keep a low profile in that class.

I hope this helps you get better grades.

Section 6: Special Skills

There are a number of special skills that will help you do better in school. If you can learn to read faster, it will help you get through your homework in less time. Improving your memory is also an important skill to have. Note taking and organizing your time better also can help you get better grades.

Chapters in this section:

1. Special Homework Skills
2. Reading Faster
3. Feedback on Reading
4. Speak to Your Class with Confidence
5. Feedback on Speaking

Special Skills

Special Homework Skills

Homework usually consists of reading material in your text book and doing written assignments. Sometimes you must do outside research on a subject.

You want to be able to read the material rapidly, understand what you read and remember important points. Then you must answer questions, solve problems or write out reports. You want to go through each area quickly and efficiently. You want to improve your skills to increase your effectiveness in these areas.

Reading faster

It is worthwhile to look into ways to increase your reading speed. Why plod along, when you can go through your homework, reading twice at fast?

Methods to increase your reading speed include skim reading before you do serious reading and clumping words together instead of reading one word at a time. At the very least, simply concentrating on reading faster will help you improve your speed and comprehension.

Understanding what you read

Most textbook material consists of important points followed by details and examples. If the material is very difficult to read, you may have to read it over several times.

Use highlighter

Some students use a highlighter to mark what they feel is important points or sentences in the book. I never liked to do that, in case I marked the wrong sentence. Also, it might make it difficult to sell the book at a later time.

Special Skills

Write important points
I feel that writing out the important points works better, because you remember what you write, and you can add other comments or thoughts. Also, writing can help the understanding process.

Experiment with what method works the best for you.

Improving your memory
People with what they call "photographic memories" are supposed to be able to remember everything they see or read. A good memory would make things a lot easier when it comes time to answer questions in class or when taking a test.

There are methods and tricks to improve your memory. One of them is to be observant and notice things around you. Another good technique is to make associations with familiar things you can visualize.

Writing down key points helps the memory for some students. Other students find that verbalizing the material or explaining it to friends ingrain the material into the memory.

Again, you can try different ways that work best for you.

Summary
Since homework usually consists of reading material in your textbook and doing written assignments, you want to be able to read the material rapidly, understand what you read and remember important points. You want to improve your skills to increase your effectiveness in these areas.

Reading Faster

Students often must read and comprehend a tremendous amount of material. Being able to read rapidly is an important skill that will make schoolwork easier, as well as help you advance in your career. Most speed-reading methods are based on skim reading first and in reading groups of words. It takes discipline and a mind-set to become a super reader.

Speed is important

It certainly is more enjoyable to be able to read something rapidly, instead of spending what seems like forever struggling through the words.

Students and workers improve

Besides the enjoyment factor, students need to get through a lot of reading material in as fast a time as possible. Efficient reading skills will help them in their schoolwork and help to improve their grades.

Workers must read reports, as well as research material, for their jobs. If they can read faster, with greater comprehension, their chance of a raise and a promotion is increased. Note that top executives usually have rapid-reading skills.

Improves comprehension

Although it is difficult to speed-read a complex chapter in a Mathematics book, using speed-reading techniques do help to improve your comprehension. This is especially true when you have to read a large amount of material that can numb your brain.

Special Skills

Skim reading

Some speed reading methods have you first skim-read the material and then read it over a second time more carefully, but yet still at high speed. In skim reading you often just scan through the material, letting your eyes catch key words, which give you the crux of the written material.

Skim several times

When reading extensive material, you can first skim over the chapter and section titles to give you an idea of when the material is about. Then quickly scan through the material again to get a better idea of the topic. Finally, you read the assignment, but still reading rapidly.

Read first sentence

Since often the first sentence of each paragraph states the main idea of that paragraph, while the other sentences elaborate on that idea, you can skim read by just reading the first sentences. In some cases, you can get enough information by only reading the first sentence from each paragraph.

Unfortunately, some writers make their paragraphs so long, that they have several ideas in them, and others stick the important sentences in the middle. In such cases, you can't use the first sentence method effectively.

Complex reading

With some complex reading—like Mathematics—you should still skim over the material, quickly looking at section titles and the equations and formulae. After you get an idea of what the material is about and where it is going, you can read it more carefully. Since you often may have to work out problems with a pencil, obviously your reading speed will not be as high as other type of reading.

Grouping words

Most people read one word at a time, saying the word to themselves. This is a slow way of doing the task, especially when your mind is capable of processing information at a much higher rate.

Look at groups of words

One of the primary tricks in speed-reading is to look at phrases and groups of words instead of individual words. Instead of reading word-by-word, you read in chunks of information. You don't have to say the word to understand what it means.

Practice with newspaper

Try reading several words, a phrase, or even a sentence at a time. A good way to practice this is to read newspaper articles by scanning down the column, digesting all the words across, instead of reading each word at a time. A newspaper column usually has 4 or 5 words per line, and you should be able to process all of them at once.

This method is one of the best for getting used to reading phases instead of words. Just practicing reading this way should noticeably increase your speed.

Summary

If you think about reading faster, you will make an effort to pick up the pace. Reading speed is something you must work on and concentrate on until it becomes a habit.

Being able to read and comprehend the material at high speed is a skill that is worthwhile for students and people in business. Most methods involve reading chunks of information so that you are skimming or scanning the book or document.

Special Skills

Feedback on Reading

Students from around the world send email to the *School for Champions* with questions and comments on various aspects of getting good grades in school. The following letters concern skills in reading faster. Note that the letters have not been edited for correct grammar or spelling.

Failed test because I can't read fast enough

Question
November 19

I am taking an exam in 3 weeks that I have failed once because I could not read and comprehend fast enough. I need help ASAP. Please

Thanks

Tina - **USA**

Answer
Some can read faster by following along with their fingers. Others seek out key words. And others mouth the words while they read. All methods can help.

If you know what material will be covered and understand the concepts, it should be easier to go through it more rapidly.

Above all, don't get nervous and try too hard. Have the feeling that you are well prepared for the test and try to be very methodical in going through it. But also, keep an eye on your watch, so that you can pace yourself.

I hope you will do well and pass the test this time.

Special Skills

Gets a pain from concentrating

Question
September 13

I'm in class 12th. I tried your advice, but got accustomed of two habit ...in one try to read with concentration but this creating the toothache physically (higher concentration but pain) ...in second no pain but poor concentration. Tell me which one is better

Also tell me if a person has not the good reading skill, how skimming will help him. Will not it aggravate the condition?

Saurabh Shyug - **India**

Answer
Some people may clench their jaw or grit their teeth when they try to concentrate too hard. That could cause a toothache. That may mean you are trying to concentrate too hard. You need to use other methods.

Although concentration is important in being able to read faster, it is only one part of the solution. One thing to realize is that you need to quickly know and understand the words to be able to read rapidly. If the words are easy, then you don't want to read slowly. Easy material should be read rapidly. But if there are many difficult words, then you need to read slower in order to understand the material.

The best thing to do is to practice reading fast when you understand most of the words. A good place to practice is when you are reading a fiction story or things in the magazines.

Since you want to improve your reading skills and be able to quickly go through material you need to read, you should try to improve your understanding of various new words. Note that many intelligence tests check your vocabulary, so it is a good area in which to improve. Mark or write down words you do not

Feedback on Reading

understand. You can use a small dictionary to check the meaning of the word. Another way is to use your word processor Thesaurus feature that will give the meanings for you. Although doing this is extra work, it is worthwhile in the future, as you will greatly improve your reading and grades.

If you are good at reading, skimming can speed up the process, because it is a good method to pick out key words and get an idea of what the material is about. Even if you can't read well, skimming and then reading more carefully can help.

I hope these ideas help you in reading faster and becoming a champion in school.

Following the lecturer in class

Question
September 12

Please give me information about sleep and reading, writing when the lecturer is teaching and just listening

Kusasira - **Uganda**

Answer
Sometimes a teacher or lecturer can be so boring that you may feel like falling asleep. One way to help you pay attention is to take notes and write down key items that are being taught. This is much better than just listening, because it forces you to follow along. Also, the notes are good for when you study for a test.

Special Skills

Confused about speed reading

Question
April 11

I have read some speed reading books by several different authors and besides a few points they seem to all agree that speeds far superior than normal speed (like at least a few thousand wpm) could be achieved. But most of them really don't provide the means of doing so, they just tell you to do a few eye movement exercises, use your hands to guide your eyes (which I don't really understand because some author advocate it and some say it's useless), then you are on your own.

Also, besides these authors the vast majority of materials on reading don't cover speed, and those do are actually very skeptical to completely denying speed reading saying it's just skimming and not "reading" (I am guessing they define reading as sub-vocalizing words in your head). My question is: 1. is there basis for speed reading? 2. is a lot of practice necessary to raise my reading speed? 3. if speed reading is possible, what are the rules to follow in practicing it?

Wilson - **USA**

Answer
I know that several methods advocate scanning along with your finger. I'm not sure if that works better. I guess it works for some, if you get used to it.

It is worth taking a quick look at the material to get an idea of what it is about before reading.

If you look at a group of words, as opposed to individual words, the major words pop out, while you ignore minor words such as "a", "the", "in", etc. That is the most important part of speed-reading. Some say that speed-reading is skimming. But there is nothing wrong with that.

Much depends on how complex the material is that you read. You can skim or read a fiction piece quickly, missing many words but still getting the story. There is often a lot of "fluff" in fiction. But reading a science book or something with complex concepts requires concentration and thought. You really can't speed-read such material. But if you have learned to read faster, you can go through the material quicker than the average person.

I will often just read the first sentence in a paragraph and then quickly skim the rest of the paragraph. Often that works well.

By concentrating on reading faster and by looking at groups of words, you can increase your speed. It is on-the-job practice.

You can try what you see in the books, but also try what suits you the best. Everyone is different and reads different types of material.

Best wishes in increasing your reading speed.

How can foreign students improve reading?

Question
November 18

How can students of foreign language improve their reading speed and comprehension?

Farhad Asl - **Iran**

Answer
Comprehension is the most important. If you can't understand, it does not matter how fast you can read. Just like children learn to comprehend what they read by starting with simple books and moving to more advanced material, students of a foreign language can do the same.

Special Skills

Once they comprehend material at a given level, they can start to read it at a faster rate, using common speed-reading techniques.

How can you not sound words while reading?

Question
July 26

Reading some articles about speed-reading I find the most difficult to understand the fact that one should not sound words while reading.

How to do not to sound words while reading?

David Vega - **Nicaragua**

Answer
Surprisingly, you can glance at a group of words and get the meaning without looking at a single word at a time. It does take a little practice, and the words must be simple enough. Try skimming down a column in a newspaper to get the gist or rough idea what you read.

Still says words to herself

Question
February 22

Thank you that helps I look at every word and say it to myself. I don't know how to stop though. I can skim for a little while but then before I know it I'm reading and saying each word again. I will look in to getting some of the suggested materials.

Thank you,

Paige - **USA**

Feedback on Reading

Answer

It is tough not to read every word. In some difficult books, you almost have to, in order to understand the material. But in much reading, you can move through it faster to get the gist of what is written.

The big thing is to practice, especially in easy-to-read material like magazines and the newspaper. Best wishes on being a rapid reader.

What if you can't read that good?

Question
November 19

I have a question? What if you can't read that good but when you try to read, people make fun of you! I try to tell my parents about this but I'm afraid they will be mad! So what do you think about all of this? What should I do?

Lexi - **USA**

Answer
I just sent you another email on this subject, saying to talk to your teacher for advice and that you don't like others to laugh at you. It probably is good to hold off on telling your parents until you see what the teacher does.

If the teacher does not care to help or to stop the kids from laughing at you, then you probably will have to tell your parents. I am sure they don't want you to be teased like that in school.

To help with your reading, find some simple books or magazines to read that are also enjoyable. If you read stuff you enjoy reading (as opposed to schoolwork reading) your skills will improve.

Best wishes on improving your reading and on stopping them from laughing at you.

Special Skills

Speak to Your Class with Confidence

Have you ever had to speak in front of your class—perhaps to give a report—and you got real nervous? Perhaps you stammered, started to sweat and even started to shake. Many students have this problem. In fact, the fear of speaking in front of a group is one of the worst fears people have. It even ranks above the fear of death (but not as great as the fear of snakes).

> When I was in high school, I was terrified of speaking in front of the class. I would tremble and my mouth would fill with saliva. The only way I could effectively give a presentation was to sit in a chair when I was in front of the class. My English teacher frowned on this and thought I was just trying to be different or difficult.

I later learned to have confidence when speaking in front of a group. Sure, there was a little nervousness, but I then was able to speak without fear.

What are you afraid of?

One big reason students get so nervous when they have to speak in front of their class is because they have a fear of looking stupid in front of their fellow students. This fear holds for all people, when they have to speak in front of others.

Another major fear is that you will forget what you were going to say or that your mind will go blank, such that you will just stand there like an idiot, while everyone watches you. You fear that you will look so stupid in front of the whole class that they may laugh and make fun of you. What a terrible feeling!

Special Skills

To top it off, when you get nervous, you may get flushed in the face, start to tremble, start to sweat a lot and who knows what else. Being humiliated like this can destroy your ego and confidence. In fact, it can really ruin your day.

Tips to overcome those fears

There are several tips or tricks to use to overcome the fear of making a mistake or looking foolish when you speak to a group:

- Know your subject matter
- Know your speech
- Have a backup, in case you forget what you want to say
- Realize that the audience isn't so special
- Practice, practice, practice

In the following material, I will explain each of those points.

Know your subject matter

If you are going to speak to the class about something, you should know the subject matter thoroughly. Since it is usually something you have just been studying, you should be able to answer questions from students who aren't as familiar with the subject as you.

You should always know more than the material you are presenting, so you can answer questions. Also, you must be prepared for the "smart-aleck" in class who knows the subject well and asks a question to try to stump you. There is more about this later in contingency plans.

Knowing the subject matter gives you a feeling of confidence before you give your talk.

Speak to Your Class with Confidence

Know your speech
A big fear students have is that they will forget what they were going to say, especially if they must speak without notes. You should know your speech or talk very well before presenting it in front of a class or an audience. Don't try to wing it. Rather, write it out ahead of time and practice it at least once.

Don't wing it
The worse thing in the world to do is to not be prepared and try to "wing it" by talking off the top of your head. Some students who have the "gift of gab" can pull this off, but it is really setting yourself up for failure. Speaking in front of your class is too important to take the risk of going blank and looking like a fool.

Write it out
The best thing to do is to write out what you plan to say. Some students will write a word-by-word report that they will later hand in to the teacher. Others will use an outline of the important points to cover, if that is their working style and they don't have to hand in the report.

Practice speech
One way to make sure you know the speech is to practice giving it many times before your actual presentation. Practice by yourself, in front of your friends or your parents. The more you give the speech the more confidence you get.

Tips on practicing
Try standing in the corner when you practice your speech out loud. The walls in the corner will reflect the sounds, so that you can hear how your voice sounds, a fraction of a second after you speak. It is strange, but effective.

Practice giving your talk into a tape recorder. Surprisingly, having a tape recorder running puts pressure on you to know your material.

Special Skills

Have a backup
It is worthwhile to bring along a "security blanket" or "safety net" in case something goes wrong in your presentation. For example, have your speech outlined on 3x5 cards. This is a good backup in case you have a mental lapse. Referring to your notes is certainly acceptable to refresh your memory.

Of course, though, you should be prepared enough that you don't have to completely depend on your notes for your material.

Tips on using notes
It is not good to read a talk word-for-word form a report you have written. In such a case, why not simply give out copies and let people read it for themselves?

To some degree, you must memorize what you are going to say. The best way is to highlight key words or phrases from your report. These will be cues to stimulate your memory and to guide you through your talk. You might simply put these words or phrases on 3x5 cards to refer to if you need it.

Note that your teacher should allow you to use some sort of reminder device like 3x5 cards. It is not fair to require you to completely memorize everything word-by-word, unless that is the purpose of the exercise. Check with the teacher before you use such an aid, so you don't get penalized.

Reduce fear of your audience
Speaking to important people or dignitaries can create fear in a person. This fear can be overcome by visualizing the people as not all that important.

Old trick
One old trick is to imagine that the audience is naked. Or perhaps imagine them all in clown outfits. A ridiculous image will make them seem not all that important. It is surprising how such an image can relax you.

Remember that they are just other kids and that they are there to hear what you have to say.

Consider your teacher. You don't see your teacher getting nervous in front of the class. Think of yourself in the role of a teacher. You are teaching the class something.

Have contingency plans in case of trouble
Whenever you give a demonstration or perform an experiment in front of the class, it is possible that something can go wrong. It is always good to prepare for any possible problems. At the very least, you should be able to think on your feet and get around the problems. Don't stop or seem flustered. Usually the audience or the class will be on your side.

Beware of the troublemaker
Another type of problem is the troublemaker. Some other student may try to give you a rough time or heckle you. Just as professional entertainers have comeback lines to handle unruly drunks in the audience, you need to handle the troublemaker in your class.

You don't want to appear flustered by his or her remark. Instead, have a mellow come-back, such as, "Thank you for the intelligent comment. Now, may I continue in my report?" This is a good put-down and yet shows you mean business.

Your goal is to get a good grade and not to let someone get under your skin or to get flustered by some problem. Prepare to handle them.

Practice, practice, practice
Practice is extremely important. The more you give a talk, the more automatic it becomes, the more meat it can have and the more confidence you have in your abilities to give the speech.

Practice alone, Practice in front of small groups or friends. Practice.

Special Skills

Feel confident

If you are going to have to give talks in front of your class, why not feel confident about doing it? Then you can feel like a champion when you successfully complete the task.

Make an extra effort. The more you successfully do something, the more confidence you have that you can do it again—even better.

Not only do you want to be able to get through your ordeal of talking in front of your class, you want to be able to feel confident before you do it and like a champion when you are through.

Summary

The way to overcome the fear of speaking to a group is to make sure you are well prepared, have some backup material ready in case you forget your lines, visualize your audience as not so important, and practice as much as you can before you speak.

Feedback on Speaking

Students from around the world send email to the *School for Champions* with questions and comments on various aspects of getting good grades in school. The following letters concern speaking in front of the class. Note that the letters have not been edited for correct grammar or spelling.

Don't care to read boring material to class

Question
September 19

This section was really very helpful in the fact that it says your peers are just there to hear what you have to say. I also have a comment, in my own personal expirence i absolutely HATE reading something in front of an audience if its a boring report or speech, but if its about something I am interested in, then I can go up with confidence and speak easy and even make a joke or two about the subject. In fact tomorrow I have to read a 5-6 minute report in front of my literature class, normally I would be really nervous but since my class lacks students or doesn't have many peers in my class (only about 15-18 people) this makes my report much easier.

I just have one more comment, my worst fear is that i would go up to the front of the class, stammer my words or just forget something completely, so what advice would you have for a person like me with this problem?

Rob – **USA**

Special Skills

Answer
Since you may not always have a choice in reading something of interest—say in a business or job situation—it is necessary to learn to make the boring interesting to you and to the audience. You are like an actor playing a role and must make sure the audience gets something out of it.

Keeping with the acting metaphor, in stage plays they often have a prompter who helps the actors when they forget their lines. In our lessons on overcoming the fear of speaking, we recommend using 3x5 cards with key words written on them as a safety net, in case the speaker's mind goes blank. Also using visual aids can help the speaker to keep on track.

Best wishes in your speaking and reading.

Afraid that others will make fun

Question
September 19

I have a problem I'm a freshman in class and I'm usually really quiet in class, so people think i don't talk. But i don't want to be like this I am not quiet i talk, but I'm shy to call out in class or raise my hand because i think people will make fun of me what should i do?

(no name given) - **USA**

Answer
I would certainly hope that the teacher would not allow others to make fun if a student gave an incorrect answer. Also note that students in high school are more mature than in middle school, where they seem to make fun of others more often.

Feedback on Speaking

The first thing you should do is to think in terms of your own grades. The student who raises his or her hand in class will usually get better grades than one who doesn't participate. So, your motivation should be to improve your grade.

In order to build up your confidence, try to pick questions that you really know the answer. If you are called on and can answer it, give yourself a silent praise: "Great job!" If you happened to be wrong, tell yourself that you will do better the next time. If someone does try to make fun of you, realize that he is a complete idiot.

I hope these ideas help. Start raising your hand and let's get some top grades in school.

Motivates self with chocolate

Question
May 27

A tip for kids is to help them is on its way for its me because a tip is just picture some thing like me for instance i love chocolate so much all I have to do and you could ton is just picture some thing that u love for example I have to do my biography report tomorrow and all I have to do is say to my self do this now like and just get it done with and then I can have all the chocolate in the world see easy huh well got to go now

Kameko - **USA**

Answer
Thanks for sharing your tip. Motivation yourself with something you really like is a good idea.

Special Skills

Extremely nervous before speaking

Question
November 5

I am an EXTREMLY nervous person I read what you have to say but i feel it wont help, I shake specially my neck and I turn pale as white paper almost as if I will faint, words wont come out of my mouth this is my worst fear, to present in front of the class, 40 students juniors and seniors its scary please, give me some fantastic and great advice that will help me on my HUGE presentation coming up.

Neelam - **USA**

Answer
Some ideas to help you are:

First of all, make your presentation simple, so it is easy to say and remember. Practice your presentation until you really know it. Have some practice sessions in front of your family and in front of your friends.

Next make some plans if you forget or go blank. Have some notes of an outline. Also have a closing line available, such as "That concludes my presentation" to use in an emergency. People won't know that you ended early.

If you can use some presentation materials like projector images or even material written on the board, it can help you focus on that and not so much on the audience.

Before you go into class, picture everyone smiling and anxious to hear what you have to say, just as if they are your good friends. It is true that they want you to do well, so you don't have to try to make a big impression.

Feedback on Speaking

I know that before you are called on to speak, your heart will be beating a mile a minute. Just concentrate on your beginning. When you area called on, count to 10 to yourself before getting up. Then when you get in front of the class, again count to 10. This puts you in control.

Start the speech by aiming it directly at the teacher or at some friend in the front. Then when you get going, you can start aiming it at others in the audience.

I hope these ideas help, and I am sure you will overcome your anxiety and do fine.

Learned how not to be nervous

Question
October 21

I used to get very nervous in front of the class. Then I just thought it through and realized that there really was nothing to be nervous about because its not like the students in my class were going to remember if I did a very bad job on my presentation/ report. I find it helpful if I volunteer to go first because that shows that you are confident and usually the teacher is a little less harsh on you if you go first. Also, if you go first, the audience is probably not even paying very close attention to what you are saying because they are interested in their own report and not making a fool of themselves.

Meghan - **USA**

Answer
Thanks for your good feedback. You certainly analyzed the situation and look like you are on the way to becoming a champion in school.

Special Skills

Will have to make presentations next year

Question
June 3

next year i will be gewtting out of the recorse room. Its with kids who have learing problems. Anyway i havent presentes in front of a big caklss and i just am to afraid to but next year i heard that we will be presenting alot. all i want to do is beable to present with out being a fraid is there any other ways you can help me? i hvae the hole summer to get rid of this fear. email me bac. thank you.

scincerly,afraid - **USA**

Answer
First write a short presentation—like one page—about a subject. A good topic is to tell about a vacation you had. Practice reading it aloud a few times to yourself. Then make some practice presentations to a few friends or family. This will get you comfortable in speaking before people.

When you have to do it in front of your class, you might use the blackboard to write certain words during your talk, just like the teacher may do. Writing helps to relieve some of your nervousness.

Remember that everyone is afraid and everyone wants to see you do a good job. I am sure you will be a champion in giving presentations next year.

Feedback on Speaking

Kids liked speech but teacher didn't

Question
April 14

I followed all of your instructions. I stayed calm, I was ready, I spoke my speech fluently, made hardly any reference to the speech, used some improvisation to refer to real life incidences. All of my peers said my speech was a level 4 for oral and visual comm. Why did my teacher give me a level 2?

(no name given) - **USA**

Answer
This is a problem when a speech is judged. The audience may like it, but the judge (in this case the teacher) didn't. It may have been the subject matter or who knows what?

You might ask the teacher to explain why you received a level 2, so that you can improve the next time. Don't complain about your grade, but just seek out information to improve, so that you will get a better grade next time.

Afraid to even speak to friends

Question
January 20

EVERY EVERY time I speak in front of the class or even sometimes with my friends i get very nervous. My mouth feels up with saliva and I always pause in my speech the more i think about it the more I get scared about it. THIS always happens I need some help with this please get back to me soon. Thanks.

Mike - **USA**

Tricks for Good Grades

Special Skills

Answer

Start with the situation of getting nervous speaking to friends. It is because you are trying to impress them—even subconsciously? In such situations where you get uptight when talking to friends, back off and slow down. Take the focus off you and what you are trying to say and put the focus on the other people. Try to take interest in what friend is saying and concentrate on listening. You don't need to say anything all the time. In fact, others prefer to have a person listen to them.

One thing you can do with friends is to try a mini-speech on them. Just as in a regular speech, you have an introduction, body and close. You could try something like this:

- **Introduction:** "Let me ask you a question."
- **Body:** "What do you think of bla bla bla?"
- **Close:** "That sounds good. Thanks."

Although your friend won't know it, you just gave something like a mini-speech.

If you can feel comfortable with that, you can start to apply it to speaking in front of your class. The thing is that when you are going to speak in front of your class, be sure you are prepared and know what you will say. Have it written down. Take your time and think in terms of communicating clearly so that everyone will understand. You are not trying to impress anyone. Rather you are communicating information. Use the blackboard to write down key words. That is what the teacher does, and it gives you a chance to catch your breath. Finally, recall how your mini-speech went with your friends. You're just doing the same thing.

It is a tough problem, but I hope these ideas will help. Let me know how things turn out.

Feedback on Speaking

Has stuttering problem

Question
December 1

I have a stuttering problem. I have had it all my life and it is very difficult to talk to people. I can't even read in front of people. To make it worse my own mother makes me so nervous that I can't even get a sentence out of my mouth. Even the people at school make me nervous. I really don't talk to anyone I'm just a quiet person and I don't talk to anyone; because I'm afraid that people will laugh at me. I come home crying almost every day because I am afraid.

What I would love is to be able to talk and read in front of people without having to study or practice anything.

Jessica - **USA**

Answer
There is a popular singer named Mel Tillis who has a stuttering problem. To listen to him try to talk is almost painful. But when he sings, he has perfect diction. That is because he knows what he will be saying in the song, whereas when he talks, he must think of what he will say and that doesn't work well for him. What is cool is that he admits he has a stuttering problem and people accept that.

If you had to recite something you memorized, I would guess it would be much easier than simply speaking to the class or reading in front of them. There are many students without a stuttering problem who get tongue-tied when trying to read in front of the class. In fact, look at the problems President Bush has with getting his words tangled.

It is a challenge when you have difficulty speaking clearly, but you can adapt and make the best of the situation. Speaking slowly and carefully does help to a degree, but if you're with a group

Special Skills

of kids who are all talking at once, it makes it extremely difficult for a careful speaker to be heard. You have to pick and choose when you want to talk.

One thing to do when you are with other kids is to be an active listener. Everyone likes someone who takes interest in what they have to say. They will usually take time to listen to your remarks without judgment concerning your stuttering. Certainly, your friends don't think less of you because you stutter.

No matter if a person stutters, is too tall or wears the wrong shoes, there will be small-minded people who make fun of the person. They usually do that to build themselves up. You shouldn't worry about anyone laughing at you. If it ever happens, just feel bad for the person who is so ignorant.

It sounds like your mother talks a lot and talks fast. Let her know it makes you nervous when you can't get a chance to talk. She loves you, but she should also be patient enough to listen to what you have to say.

Look at all the good things you can do and be proud of it. Accept the fact you have this speaking challenge. But don't give up on it. Public speakers practice, practice, practice until seems like it is second nature to them. Look at the biography of the ancient Greek Demosthenes who had a stuttering problem and went on to be a great orator:

I'm sure you can learn to better cope with your stuttering problem and excel in what you do, just like a champion. Best wishes, and let me know how things turn out.

Can't stand in front of class

Question
August 27

Well I read your site and I cant get up in front of people at all I cant even stand at the front of the class and not cry that's my one main thing that I do it I cry and I cant help and I'm in the 8th grade and its getting to be a really embarrassing thing to me because people are starting to make fun of me and Id really like to know how to solve this problem so please help me

Keely - **USA**

Answer
The reason most people get nervous when in front of a group is that they are afraid of looking foolish. But what happens is that getting so nervous just makes them feel worse about it.

What you need to do is to start off slowly and have a series of successes to build up your confidence.

First of all, you might tell your teacher that you get very nervous speaking in front of the class, but you are trying to overcome that fear a little at a time. Perhaps the teacher will help you.

Can you think of ways where you could go up in front of the class to do something without having to talk—like bringing some papers to the teacher or perhaps writing something on the board? If you can do that successfully, give yourself a pat on the back and say, "Yes! Good job!" It is doing little things like that and celebrating that will build up your confidence.

When you talk with some friends, you don't get nervous, do you? But if there are some other kids along in the group, you might feel a little nervous. Think of every time you talk with other kids as mini-speeches. It is as if you are in front of a very small group. Again, congratulate yourself after the success.

Special Skills

When you do have to go in front of the class again, take a deep breath before you go up, count to at least 5 before you start talking, and aim your talking at some good friend in the class. Don't even think about the other kids. Keep is short, go back, and say to yourself, "Good job" even if it wasn't all that good.

I hope these ideas help. It isn't fun to be so nervous and afraid, but I'm sure you have the courage to overcome this challenge and become a champion in talking in front of a group. Just remember to practice a little at a time. If you have some trouble, take a step back and try again.

Let me know how things turn out.

Suddenly fearful

Question
August 24

I am 15 years old, going to be a sophomore. This past year, all of the sudden i had a fear of speaking in front of a group of people. Even reading out loud from a textbook made my heart beat so fast, and my voice shook when I read. I don't know what to do! When I even think about having to say anything in front of a class or group I get so nervous. I haven't talked to anyone about this, but do I need a psychiatrist? Please help me!

Margaret - **USA**

Answer
There is a lot of pressure when you're in front of the class, even if you're just reading something. You don't want to make a mistake, have your mind go blank or look like an idiot in front of all your classmates. It is a great fear of many people and is nothing unusual.

But it is also something you would want to improve upon. It's OK to be a little nervous, but you don't want it to affect you.

Feedback on Speaking

Some things you might try are:

1. Every time you raise your hand to answer a question in class or if the teacher asks you a question, think of it as a mini-speech in front of the class. It is good practice. Pat yourself on the back, after you answer, and say, "Good job."

2. Try to get a chance to get in front of the class for some small items. Like if you could help the teacher hand out papers and make an announcement to the class. Small items where you can sit down right away can help build your confidence. You might even let your teachers know you get nervous and are trying to overcome the problem.

3. Always take your time and remember the other kids (or most of them) are on your side.

Special Skills

Section 7 — Learning and Teaching

Sure there are all sorts of tricks to get good grades, but the real thing is that you want to be able to learn something in school. What good does it do you to have great grades, if you really didn't learn the material? Next semester the teacher may say, "As you should have learned in your previous class." And you will say, "Huh?"

We've included some basic ideas to help you learn what you have been taught. One of the best ideas is to try to explain what you've learned to someone else or to try to teach the person. That really reinforces what you have learned and brings out the things you need to learn.

Chapters in this section are:

1. Learn to Get Good Grades by Observing Others
2. Get Better Grades by Teaching Others

Learn to Get Good Grades by Observing Others

Besides learning the subject matter in school, your goal is to also get good grades. Being smart helps, but knowing the techniques for getting good grades can allow you to even surpass those who have more natural ability than you.

By studying and observing what other students do—especially those who seem to be excelling in getting good grades—you can gain valuable information on how to do better in school.

Learn from observation

People who want to improve in some endeavor will often watch and observe others in order to learn techniques that can help them excel.

Athletes

Professional athletes often spend time watching videos of the top players to learn techniques they use and to see what special characteristics—beyond pure talent—that give them an edge.

Writers

Writers will read the works of great authors, not for the sake of being entertained, but to study the techniques used in presenting a good story in print.

Students

Getting good grades requires special skills and techniques that are not generally taught. You can remain oblivious to these skills and just get by or you can try to give yourself an advantage in school. One way to learn those techniques is by observing what good students and bad students do to get the grades they receive. You can learn from observing others.

Learn from the winners
Observe the students who are doing well in school, especially those who don't seem much smarter than you. Don't look at who they are. Rather, look at what they do.

Forget the class brain
One thing is not to bother observing the class brain, the rich kid or the person who is real good looking. They may be succeeding in school for reasons over which you have no control. You can't learn many lessons from them.

Good study habits
Instead, study the student who has certain study habits, who knows how to deal with the teacher, and who has confidence in his or her ability. You can learn the things these students are doing to succeed in school. Often they aren't the smartest or the hardest working, but they just seem to be able to excel.

Positive character traits
Being able to deal on a positive basis with the teacher is an invaluable skill. Some do it by being the "teacher's pet" and are hated by everyone else. Instead of imitating those students, look to those who have positive character traits that are appealing.

Learn from the losers
You can also learn from the students who are not doing well in school. Don't pick the kids who are not too bright or who have some learning disability. Their lack of getting good grades may not be their fault.

Rather, observe those who have the ability but who have bad attitudes, who have negative character traits, or who do things that cause them to get poor grades.

Study them. Then, **don't do that!**

Learn to Get Good Grades by Observing Others

You've seen the students who drag into class late, showing an attitude that they hate to be in class. You've seen the ones who smart off to the teacher. And you know some who say they hate doing homework and don't bother with it. They are good examples NOT to follow, since they usually get poor grades or—if they are talented—less than their potential.

Summary

A goal in school is to get good grades. Knowing the techniques for getting good grades can allow you to even surpass those who have more natural ability than you. By studying and observing what other students do, you can gain valuable information on how to do better in school.

Learning and Teaching

Get Better Grades by Teaching Others

A good way to help in learning a subject matter—and thus getting better grades—is to teach the material to others. This forces you to review the material and also reinforces it in your memory.

One way to informally teach others is to simply explain the material to your friends or other students who are having trouble with the lessons. Statistics show that you learn more by teaching others.

How can teaching others help?

It is well know that when you explain or try to teach a subject to someone else, you learn it better yourself. A big problem with learning things in class is that shortly afterwards much of the material is forgotten. Studies say that soon after you learn something in class 80% is forgotten.

You can recall better

Although you seem to forget what you've learned in class—such that your mind goes blank about some things when you take a test—the information is still really hidden in your brain. You may not be able to dredge up the answers on a test, but it is surprising how you can recall these things when you try to explain them to another person—even years later.

You learn by verbalizing

When you verbalize information, you are using another part of your brain, and this increases your ability to understand and remember the information.

You organize your thoughts
Another good thing about trying to explain a subject matter to another person is that it helps you organize your thoughts. Any questions or misunderstandings you may have had will come to light when you have to explain the subject yourself. Often you must work things out in your mind in order to properly explain them to someone else.

It makes you feel better
Another benefit of helping others learn is that it makes you feel better about yourself and the contribution you are making to making the world a better place.

Who can I teach?
Finding someone to teach or explain the subject to can be a challenge. Even finding someone to discuss the subject, so you can verbalize what you have learned, is often not easy.

Friends and classmates
One thing you can do is to try to explain study material to your friends. You can even take turns in teaching each other to reinforce your knowledge. Teaching each other on a regular basis can even be part of doing your homework together.

Some schools have programs
Some schools have programs where students go to last year's class to help teach the younger kids. They often listen to someone a year or two older better than to the teacher, so they learn better. And of course, the student doing the teaching refreshes his or her knowledge of the material.

Although this will not directly improve your grades in classes you are presently taking, knowing last year's material better will give you a better background for this year's work.

Get Better Grades by Teaching Others

Guaranteed better grades?

Will you be guaranteed of getting better grades if you teach others? You probably will know the subject better and thus do better in class and on tests, but unfortunately there are no guarantees in life. You just do the best you can.

But I believe it will help.

Summary

Verbalizing your knowledge, explaining lessons to others and teaching what you have been studying are good ways to learn the material better yourself. Teaching last year's material gives you a better background for this year's work.

Getting a better understanding about your subjects should help you get better grades in those classes. Besides that, it can be fun to help others learn what you know.

Section 8: Personal Improvement

The final area in this book concerns personal improvement. We have five major areas in your life that are important for succeeding in school, in dealing with other people and in life in general.

We also mention the area of hyperactivity, which is a problem that plagues some students.

Chapters in this section are:

1. Achieving Your Goals
2. Being Healthy
3. Feedback on Health
4. Being Knowledgeable
5. Being Excellent
6. Feedback on Excellence
7. Good Character
8. Being Valuable
9. Harness Your Hyperactivity
10. Feedback on Hyperactivity

Personal Improvement

Achieving Your Goals

A champion is a person who can achieve a difficult goal or overcome challenging obstacles. The difficult goal could be winning the state championship, getting an "A" in Chemistry or getting a date with some special person. Challenges could be overcoming the fear of speaking to a group, reducing your weight or coping with a mean teacher. Once you set a goal of what you want to do or get, there is a simple procedure to follow to achieve that goal. Afterwards, it is good to give thanks and give back.

Setting your goal

Often goals are an effort to solve a problem or something you have to do. If you had a test tomorrow, your goal would be to study enough to pass the test. If you were attacked by a giant bear, your goal would be to get away to safety.

Other goals are seeking something that will give you pleasure or enjoyment. You might want to make some money, so you could buy a new MP3 player. Or you could seek to get a straight-A average, so you will get a college scholarship.

For most of your goals, you aren't even aware of them. You don't purposely set a goal to buy a candy bar and enjoy eating it. You just do it. But for major goals that may take a lot of effort, it is essential to define the goal and to write it down.

Achieving the goal

The steps to achieve your goal are:

1. Get some support

2. Get a good idea or plan of action

3. Have a Champion attitude

Personal Improvement

4. Take a shot

5. Celebrate or re-evaluate

1. Get some support
Although you can do things completely by yourself, it is always good to include others in your effort. They may be able to provide some help, advice or simply root for your success.

You want support, but you don't want meddling. Some students don't like to tell their parents they have some goal, because often the parents will try to take over and give unwanted help or advice. It is nice to get someone to root for you but not to play the game for you. Thus, you need to use judgment concerning to whom you tell your goals.

In school, it is not a bad idea to let your teacher know you are trying to get good grades in the class as a goal. It helps to have the support of the teacher. But also, the teacher will try to keep you from backsliding and goofing off. If you tell the teacher you are working to get good grades in the class, you had better follow through in your goal.

2. Get plan of action
Whatever your goal, you need a plan of action or means to achieve that goal. The idea of how to achieve the goal can be difficult, and you may try a number of ideas and plans until you find the one that works.

For example, if you need money, you get the idea of getting a job. You also get the idea of a way to get a job is to stand on a street corner with a sign. If that idea doesn't work, you might try looking at the want ads in the paper as a method to achieve your goal. There are also subtle strategies that can be used. During the Great Depression of the 1930s, some people would go on a job interview dressed in rags as a strategy to get sympathy to get a job when jobs were scarce.

Achieving Your Goals

Students typically want to get good grades in their classes. Some may have a plan to study late at night, while others may just do the minimum. As you get feedback on your results, you can make adjustments.

3. Have Champion attitude

You need to have the attitude of a champion to help you achieve your goal. You need motivation, confidence and energy before you get started. Once you implement your plans, you need excellence and character to assure your complete success.

Motivation

You need to be motivated to do something. The rewards or benefits you seek, as compared to the work required is your motivation.

In situations where you are dealing with other people, you need to be able motivate them to act. This is done by providing the others with something they want or value.

The saying is, "*You can get what you want by helping others get what they want.*" This is a win-win situation.

Confidence

You need to be confident that you can perform the tasks required to achieve your goal and get what you want. Confidence comes from learning what to do and how to do it, and then having some success in applying your skills. If you practice taking tests, such that you are relaxed and feel you have skill in that task, you will have more confidence in taking the final exam.

Other people should have confidence in you, such that they are sure you will come through and do what is promised.

The saying is, "*Celebrate every success, no matter how small.*"

Tricks for Good Grades

Personal Improvement

Energy
Inertia often keeps a person from starting a task, especially if it is difficult or unpleasant. You need energy to get going and to keep going. Motivation and confidence help build up that energy. But also, good physical and mental health is important. You can be motivated all you want, but if your mind isn't clear and your body is tired, you aren't going to be doing much.

The saying is, *"Take care of your health."*

Excellence
When you buy something, you want quality goods. Likewise, when you do something, you should do excellent work. When you do a good job, step back and take a look at it with pride. It is a good feeling to have pride in your work. That means you have pride in yourself. Pat yourself on the back and say, "Good job."

However, doing good work that is the wrong work is not productive. You need to know the requirements and what is really wanted.

The saying is, *"Do your best and be proud of it."*

Character
There are two main areas of character: honesty and determination. Both are important, but for different reasons.

Lying, stealing or cheating just doesn't pay. A person may advance for a while with dishonesty, but other people don't like it and will seek revenge. Once you are known as dishonest, people will not want trust you or care to deal with you. A student can cheat and get a better grade, but if he gets caught, the consequences are greater than the gain.

Reliability and responsibility fall under honesty. It is better to be admired for being reliable than to be self-centered and scorned.

Determination, courage, and perseverance are admirable character traits that will help a person achieve his or her goals and succeed.

4. Take a shot
As the commercial says, "Do it." You've got to implement your plan and seek to achieve your goal.

5. Celebrate or re-evaluate
Goals are seldom achieved with one effort. If you fail or have a setback, it is necessary to re-evaluate your plan, make adjustments and continue or give it another effort.

If you do succeed, celebrate your achievement. This makes you feel great—like a champion.

Giving back
Once you have achieved your goal, celebrated your success and reaped the benefits of your rewards, you should step back and give thanks for your good fortune. A good way to do that is to try to give back by helping others succeed. This could be to help the needy, help some fellow students or even volunteer to help your mother with some task.

Helping others is championing a cause and makes you a true champion.

Summary
By achieving a difficult goal or overcoming problems, you feel like a champion. You set goals for everything you do. You should write down the goal if it is a difficult goal. Once you set a goal of what you want to do or get, you make plans, get support, have a champion attitude, go for it, and celebrate or re-evaluate. Afterwards, it is good to give thanks and give back.

Personal Improvement

Being Healthy

Being healthy means that your body and mind function as they are supposed to. In your role as a student, it is important that you are both physically and emotionally healthy. You can't do a good job in school, if you don't feel well. Being healthy makes you feel good and allows you to perform more effectively. You can maintain your health by taking care of yourself and avoiding toxic situations.

Good health
Health concerns both physical and emotional well-being.

Physical health
Being physically healthy means that your body is functioning as it should, without pain, discomfort or lack of capabilities. Causes of ill health include injuries, disease, diet, stress and genetics. Also, poor cleanliness habits can result in illness or skin ailments.

Emotional health
Being emotionally or mentally healthy means that your mind and emotions are functioning as they should, without anxiety, depression or other malfunctions. Causes of mental ill health include physical disease, stress, genetics and mental abuse.

For example, being constantly and unfairly criticized can affect your emotional well-being. Also, sometimes depression is caused by chemical changes in your body.

Personal Improvement

Importance and benefits of good health

Having good health is important and beneficial to a student. Health is a necessity, so ill health can prevent you from doing what you want in an effective manner or at all. Good health is necessary to effectively do your schoolwork. You can't do well if you don't feel well.

Physical health

Being physically healthy is of prime importance in life. Being ill or not feeling well can drastically affect your ability to work or play. Obviously, if you feel physically healthy, you can be more productive, as well as happier in school.

Students want to exhibit vitality when they are in class and with their friends. They want to look and be healthy.

Mental health

Emotional well-being is also important. Suffering stress, depression, anxiety or other mental or emotional ailments is not fun. You would like your whole life to be happy and satisfying. It is important to be emotionally healthy in order to study effectively.

In life

School is only one part of your life. You want to be able to enjoy all aspects of your life and to live a long, productive and enjoyable life. Being healthy will also allow you to gain knowledge and skills, do excellent work, be valuable to others, and be honorable to those with whom you deal.

Maintaining health

You should take care of yourself in order to maintain your physical and mental health.

Physical health

Physical health starts with a good diet and includes sufficient exercise, as well a generally taking care of your health. Exercise is important not only for your health, but it also increases your energy and vitality. Exercise gives the type of subtle muscle tone that looks good to an audience. An out-of-shape student does not have the same credibility or appeal as one who looks fit.

Certainly, smoking should be avoided. Drinking alcohol and/or taking drugs are not only bad for your physical health, but they can result in you looking and sounding like a fool.

You should also know how to deal with illness or injury by appropriate health care.

Mental health

Maintaining mental or emotional health is not as specific as maintaining physical health. Positive reinforcement is a way to keep the right mental attitude, as opposed to thinking of things in negative terms. You also want to avoid situations that cause excess stress, or if you are in such situations, to cope with it. For example, giving a presentation in front of the class can be stressful, but excess worry is counterproductive. Good preparation and positive visualization can reduce the stress. Also, remember the adage: *"Don't sweat the small stuff. Everything is small stuff."*

Overreaction to criticism from teachers, parents or other kids can cause your stomach to churn. It is good to take such criticisms in stride, consider the source of the criticism, and try to appropriately improve.

You should be aware of these problems and try to avoid negative situations. If you can't bear the negative atmosphere around you, seek to move on to a healthier emotional environment.

Summary

You want to function properly both physically and mentally or emotionally. Unhealthy habits and stressful working conditions can affect your health, as well as your ability to study. You should take care of your health and work environment, so that you can feel good and be productive.

Feedback on Health

Students from around the world send email to the *School for Champions* with questions and comments on various aspects of getting good grades in school. The following letters concern health. Note that the letters have not been edited for correct grammar or spelling.

Healthy body

Question
September 14

What is the importance of a healthy body?

Nadia - **USA**

Answer
A person with a healthy body will usually feel better and have more energy. This can result in being able to get better grades in school.

When a person is sick, it makes it more difficult to do school work or anything.

Personal Improvement

Why is being healthy necessary?

Question
August 29

In your section about being healthy i do not understand how being healthy can fit into your education. I mean it CAN make you feel and do better but are you really trying to say that staying healthy and fit is one of the 5 things to be smart. Just because you are not healthy will not affect your education or your grades.

I'm in grade 8.

Kevin - **USA**

Answer
Health is a major concern of all people. When a person is sick or has a health problem, it makes it more difficult to concentrate on other things, such as work or school. That is why it is important for a person to take care of his or her health.

A student with a disability or continual health problem has a greater challenge to overcome. But it doesn't mean that the student can't do well in school and even excel. In some cases, students with such problems actually become stronger, such that they do better than the others who have no health problems.

There is also an attitude issue. Almost everyone has some ailment or area that not function as it should. Some say, "I am unhealthy," while others will say, "I'm healthy, but I've just got some problems I have to overcome." The positive attitude is better.

Being Knowledgeable

In your role as a student, it is important that you are both knowledgeable in your subject matters and skilled in study techniques.

Your ability to study effectively is enhanced with knowledge and skill, resulting in better grades. Being able to understand things and perform tasks can make you feel confident and good about yourself. You gain knowledge through study and skill through application of what you learned.

Knowledge and skill

Being a knowledgeable student means you are well informed about subject matters and studying techniques. A student who has insufficient knowledge does not know what he or she is talking about and does not know how to succeed in school.

Being skilled in school means you have mastered study techniques and are able to do work and take tests in an effective manner.

Some students specialize in one or two subjects, to an extreme. If it is about science or computers, they are often called nerds. If it is only about sports, they are called jocks. My feeling is that it is good to be mildly knowledgeable about as many subjects as you can.

Importance and benefits

It is much easier to go to school if you thoroughly know the subject matter and are skilled in study techniques. Lack of knowledge can result in anxiety and embarrassment. A knowledgeable student will usually get better grades.

Personal Improvement

A student who is skillful in study techniques will know how readily do homework and prepare for a test. A skilled student can often overcome a lack of knowledge through his or her studying ability.

Confidence and esteem, plus better grades, are some of the rewards from being knowledgeable and skilled.

Become knowledgeable

You should make sure that you become knowledgeable and skilled. The way to gain knowledge in school is to observe, study and read. Good students are known to be voracious readers. Being curious and interested in many things helps you to become knowledgeable about them.

Applying what you have learned and also analyzing the results of your work are good ways to establish your skills.

You need to be healthy and alert to be able to learn and gain skills. You also need to do excellent work, as well as to have character to become knowledgeable. Getting a reputation for your knowledge and skill can lead to becoming admired and valuable.

Summary

You should be both knowledgeable in your subject matters and skilled in study techniques. This will result in better grades, as well as making you feel confident and good about yourself. You gain knowledge through study and skill through application of what you learned.

Being Excellent

If you know you did your best, you are excellent. In your role as a student, it is important that you do your best and produce excellent work. This will increase your confidence and esteem, as well as result in praise and other benefits. Excellence requires satisfying the homework requirements and even going beyond what is expected.

Excellence

Doing an acceptable job in your schoolwork means that you have completed the assignment as required, it was turned in on time, and it was without errors or omissions. On the other hand, doing an excellent job means you have done your best and have exceeded the expectations of the teacher.

To some degree, excellence is in the eye of the beholder. If you have done your best, you may feel your schoolwork is excellent. But the teacher may have had different expectations and a different way to evaluate whether or not the work was excellent. That is why it is important to know the requirements and expectations before proceeding with an assignment.

Benefits of being excellent

The benefits of doing excellent work is an increase in confidence and self-esteem, as well as recognition and praise.

Confidence and esteem

It is a good feeling when you complete a difficult school project. It can increase your confidence in being able to do even more challenging tasks.

If you have done your best, gone the extra mile and produced what you feel is an excellent assignment, you should feel proud of yourself and your abilities. It is especially gratifying if you can look at what you have accomplished with pride.

Praise
If your teacher and fellow students also feel that you have done excellent work, you may receive praise or acknowledgement for what you have done. They will recognize you as a student who does his or her best to do quality work. A student with a reputation for doing excellent work will certainly get better grades than someone who often does a shoddy job.

Become excellent
You should take care of yourself to assure excellence. The first thing in ensuring that you do excellent job is to know the requirements for completing your assignment. You must then work hard to complete the task on time and per the requirements, with no errors or omissions.

The attitude of doing excellent work goes beyond simply satisfying teacher requirements. It is delivering a product that is beyond your teacher's expectations. You should add an extra touch of quality to all of your assignments.

You need to be healthy and alert to do excellent work. You also need knowledge and skill, as well as character to complete your assignments. Having a reputation for excellence can lead to becoming admired and considered valuable by your teachers, parents, and friends.

Summary
It is good to do your best to produce excellent work. This will increase your confidence and esteem, and you may receive praise from your teachers and fellow students. Excellence requires satisfying the homework requirements and doing more than is expected.

Feedback on Excellence

Students from around the world send email to the *School for Champions* with questions and comments on various aspects of getting good grades in school. The following letters concern being excellent. Note that the letters have not been edited for correct grammar or spelling.

Used to get good grades, but they have dropped

Question
November 14

Hi. I am a grade 10 student and I used to get good marks (88s) in grade 9 and other previous grades, but in high school (gr.10-12), I am struggling with math and English (50s n 60s). Can u tell me how to get better marks in high school? Also, do universities look at your grade 10 marks? If so, do they look at your final marks or interim marks or both? Don't they only look at your grade 11 and 12 marks in Canadian universities? Holla back. Thank you.

Rouvina - **Canada**

Answer
Although school gets more difficult as you advance, your grades should not drop so much unless something else is going on. Take a look at what you have been doing to see if you have been getting sidetracked in your studies.

You want to learn to study smarter and make the most of your study time.

Personal Improvement

Talk to your Math and English teacher and ask for advice on how you can improve your grades. For one thing, it is good that they know you really care about your grades. Secondly, they may give some good pointers. Teachers want their students to do well, because it reflects on their teaching abilities.

Universities usually look at your total grade point average. Some may just look at the upper grades. But in any case, you want to do as well as possible in preparation for college. But even if you don't get top grades, there are always schools that will give you a chance.

I hope these ideas help and that you will be able to get good grades in high school and do well in college. You've already taken the first step in trying to improve your abilities.

I am a slow learner and get poor grades

Question
November 14

Hello. I live in Calgary, Alberta, Canada and I just wanted to know if the universities/ post-secondary education people look at your grade 10 marks, not just grade 11 and 12 marks? Also I used to do go in jr. high (average 88%'s), but now I'm sitting on average of 65%. I think it's because i am a slow learner and high school's pace is really fast, but could you help me how to do better in high school? Thanks.

(no name given) - **Canada**

Answer
Most colleges look at your total grade point average, but some look at just the last years. Either way, you need to improve your grades.

If you feel that the pace in high school is too fast, then you need to make some adjustments in how you work and what classes you take. The assumption in school is often that you learned some of the material in previous years, so they don't need to cover it very well. The problem is when a student was not taught the material in the lower grades or did not pay attention at that time.

Look at where your weak areas are. If the present class is too hard and you can't keep up, then you will need to take slightly easier classes. You want to be pushed and have the classes to be a challenge but not so much of a challenge that you get poor grades.

Never call yourself a slow learner. Instead consider the fact that you need to improve your study habits in various areas. If you read slowly, you can work on improving your reading speed and skills. But in the meanwhile, allocate extra time to complete the reading assignment. Everyone does not work at the same speed.

Much of learning is "catching on" to the main points. Taking notes in class is good to help you review what is said in class. You can also get an idea of what the teacher considers is important, because that will often be on a test.

I hope these ideas help you excel in school.

Moving to Canada

Question
July 21

My question is that my family is shifting to Canada. I have just given my 9th grade examinations my parents are shifting because we can get good education, as the country we are living in has no standard as compared to Canada and other countries. My ques-

Personal Improvement

tion is that what subjects I would be having in the 10th grade, I want to have some knowledge about the education system. Please tell me in detail so I can make my self-prepared.

Osama Aslam – **Pakistan**

Answer

It is smart to be prepared for the new educational system. Most cities in Canada have their own educational system and emphasize different subjects. Certainly math, science, writing and English are important.

You probably can't do anything until you actually move to the city in Canada. Then you can find out the high school where you will be going. You can then the city school board, as well as the school to ask for information on preparations you should make and what to expect.

Another thing to do is to try to find others from Pakistan who live in that city. Your parents probably will want to do this too. In this way, you can get information from people who have already settled in. Also, you might find some students your own age that can give you pointers.

One big adjustment is the different culture. People and students probably do many things differently than you are used to. It will take a little time to adjust and to get new friends.

Best wishes in your new country and new school. It will be an exciting adventure for you.

Feedback on Excellence

Others don't have to study as hard

Question
June 21

I study really hard for math test and i do well but when it comes to the exam I do not do so well and i found out that I even read more than those that even got a higher grade than I did and when I am studying they are just wasting there time doing something irrelevant. What is my problem?

Mary - **Nigeria**

Answer
It is important to do well in tests. That is a skill that will help you in all classes. See our lessons on being good in tests.

Sometimes students get too nervous in a test, and that affects their grade. You need to make sure you know what is important in class, because that is what is often in the test.

In mathematics, doing the homework is important, because being able to solve problems is considered more than memorizing things in the exams. Homework is practice for the test.

Never worry about how much other students study or how well they do. Just be concerned that you do the best job you can. Then you can be proud of yourself. If someone can get by with less studying than you in math, then good for that person. But don't concern yourself. In fact, there are other things that you can do that are better than them. So it all evens out.

I hope these ideas help you become a champion in school. I am sure you will.

Personal Improvement

Wants to do excellent before high school

Question
May 10

Hey, I go 2 grde 8, goin 2 grde 9. The problem is that...I want to do excellent this last 3rd term...grde 8 is almost comin 2 n end, n i wana go 2 a very gud high school, 2 mke my parenz proud...especially my dad, my dad sez dat if i get 4 A's/80%'z (or higher) den i get w/e i want, not only dat it mkez every1 in my family proud. I did so well in 1st term, but not in 2nd, n now diz last term i want 2 da best i can. But itz so hard 2 get 80%z n 90%z how do i go from a level 3/3+ student 2 a level 4...i'm close but i wana b da closest n do da best! How DO I MKE DIZ POSSIBLE!?!?!? I awlwayz say 2 my-self i do alwayz study, cuz datz wat my parenz wana c, but i neva get da chance 2 study. Help plz!! Plz giv me da best advice u can! I wana do DA BEST!:'(

Mugnin - **Canada**

Answer

I am glad to hear that you want to be excellent in school, because that is the start of becoming a champion in school. If you want it, then it will happen. But it may take work.

One thing is that you feel that you have done the best you can. That is important to you. But besides doing your best, you also need to use techniques that will make your work easier and more efficient.

Set aside a time for study, because that is important. You can still have time for other things, but assign your times so you will get everything done.

One big advice I have for going to high school is that you should be careful using the slang or shortcuts from instant messages and email. Although it is popular and easier, you also can get into a bad habit in using the slang and not learn how to properly spell words. A high school teacher that saw the sentence "cuz datz wat my parenz wana c" would probably give you an F. So, it is just a warning to avoid in your schoolwork.

I hope these ideas help, and best wishes in becoming the excellent student that you are able to be.

Not getting as good grades as before

Question
March 19

i used to get good marks during my school life but now i am studying in 1st year MCA but now I am not able to maintain the same standard. Now it is difficult for me to pass. Why?

Vivek Nayak - **India**

Answer
One problem is that as you get older, there are more distractions that keep you from concentrating as much. Also, classes may be getting more difficult and it is harder to understand the material. Reducing your workload may help. It is always good to ask the teacher to give some suggestion on improving your grades. Sometimes they can point out things where you can improve.

Do not get discouraged. Give yourself praise but then set goals to do better next time.

Best wishes in getting good grades and a good job.

Personal Improvement

Can't excel in math

Question
May 10

I really want to do well in school, but it's already May and final exams are a month away. They start on June 16th.

I'm in grade 9 going on to grade 10, and my teachers were telling me that universities look at grade 9 marks as well. I'm doing really poorly in math, because I find it really hard. It's a big change from grade 8 to grade 9 math. I haven't learned half the things the teacher teaches.

I have a really good teacher, but I just don't seem to understand anything. And then I don't know what questions to ask her, because I just don't seem to understand anything.

When I get home and start to do my homework, I sometimes get it, but when the test rolls around I forget how to do the questions and how to apply the formulas and things like that.

My mark in math during midterm was 56%. I'm barely passing, and I can't go to summer school, because I want to go to summer school to do grade 10 History to get a bit ahead. And this year, along with my math exam, I have a science, French and religion exam.

I'm really stressed out, and I have no idea how to improve my marks. My parents get really mad if my average isn't 80% or above, and at midterm it was 76%. I really want an 80+ average so I can get on the honor roll and make my parents proud, but math is keeping me from getting it.

I play soccer, which takes up some of my time after school for three or two days a week. And I also try to exercise to keep fit cause I'm not in too great of a shape.

Feedback on Excellence

My parents have told me to get a tutor, but I don't want to. I keep telling myself that if I really try hard enough I can get an 80, but it's just not working. When I tell myself I'm going to study for a good two hours or so, it just never happens. I say I'll study in the morning, but in the morning I'm too tired. So I say I'll study during my lunch, but it just never gets done. And when the test comes around, I'm just like it's okay if I fail this one. I'll do really well on the other one. But do I do well on the next one? No.

And now I have a month before exams, and I'm in panic mode to improve my marks. All my other marks are in the 70's and 80's, but my math mark is in the 50's, and it really makes me mad!

I've cheated on math tests by writing down the formula's sometimes. And now I'm worried that the exam is going to come, and I'm not going to know anything. I don't know how to study properly for any tests or for the tests. So if you can please, please, please help me figure something out I would be so grateful.

Kelly – **USA**

Answer

It is good that you want to do well in school, because that desire is important in succeeding. Certainly 9th grade is different than 8th, since you are now more in the "big time." Of course, the step to college is another big jump.

Math can be difficult until you really catch on and get into the flow. It consists of a number of simple rules and formulas that you combine to solve problems. The idea of math homework is often to practice combining those concepts and solving the tricky problems. Just like some people are good at playing chess, some catch on to math right away, while others have to struggle. But that doesn't mean that those that don't catch on right away should fail or do poorly. It is just a little more work involved.

Personal Improvement

Right now, you are in "crunch time", so you need to set some priorities and make some changes to make sure you get a passing grade in math, as well as good grades in the other classes. You might look at how much time soccer is taking for you and consider whether to drop out for the rest of the semester. You still want to get some exercise, because that does help your thinking abilities.

Don't be too proud to get a tutor. Your big goal is to get a decent grade in math. Getting a poor grade on your own isn't worth it. First of all, I would go to your math teacher and tell her you are concerned about your grades. Ask her if she can recommend a tutor or some other way to help your understanding. If your teacher knows you are really concerned, she may give you some special considerations.

Let your parents know that you would be willing to use a tutor. The person can help you review concepts you don't understand and help you prepare for the finals.

As far as cheating on your math test go, of course that is not a good idea. If you get caught, the stigma will follow you, plus it will affect your grades. Also, it is not the right thing to do. Another thing is not to tell anyone that you did cheat on previous tests. You shouldn't even tell your best friends, because it can slip out to someone else, and word gets around.

One thing to do is to take notes in class and write down important points the teacher makes. Good college students are dedicated note-takers. Then when you study, you can review your notes and they will help you remember things.

Trying to study a subject for two hours can actually discourage you from doing it. Break your math studying into smaller pieces and then try to blitz through them. Make sure you get something done each night instead of waiting until the morning to get started. Then it is too late.

Feedback on Excellence

I hope these ideas will help you get a better grade in math and your other subjects. I think one of the most important is to let your teacher know you want to get a better grade and to ask for some advice. Your teacher wants you to get a good grade too.

Good Character

Great people are usually judged by their character. Make sure that your character is great. Having good character means that you have such admirable traits as honesty, responsibility and courage.

It is beneficial for you to have good character. Being honorable and honest in the work you do and in your relations with others are essential in your life. Having an honorable character also provides you with personal benefits and can enhance your grades.

Having character

"Character" is sort of a catch-all word that describes your characteristic traits. If someone says you have character, it usually means that you are honorable and honest, have integrity, are courageous, and are reliable and responsible.

Poor character

On the opposite end of the spectrum, there are students who lie, cheat, or steal. They may also be lazy, unreliable or inconsiderate of others. Some are cowards.

Quite a character

The phrase "He (or she) is quite a character" usually refers to an extreme or unique personality. You can be considered quite a character if you dress and act in your own unique manner that is different than almost everyone else. You can be quite a character but still have good character by being honest, reliable and determined.

Personal Improvement

Good character important
It is obvious that honesty and integrity are important. The same is true for reliability and other forms of character, such as being courageous or brave. You should be ethical and conscientious in your work. This is especially important when working on a team.

Having an honorable character is a natural progression from being healthy, skilled, excellent and valuable in school.

Benefits
Being a student of good character is important in your relationship with your teachers and other students, as well as your own self-worth.

Respected
If you are known as an honest and honorable student, as well as a person who is reliable and responsible, you will be respected by those with whom you deal. Fellow students, teachers and your parents will trust you, know they can depend on you, and want you involved in their activities.

People don't like to deal with someone who lies, steals or is lazy. Even your best friend can be turned off by such behavior.

Esteem and virtues
Another important factor is that the honorable student has a greater self-esteem. You feel good about yourself. Finally, there is the religious aspect of having the virtues of honesty, morality and ethics.

Maintain character
You should take care of yourself to insure that you have good character. Your actions determine what people think of you and establish your reputation. They also determine how others will respond to what you do and say.

The way to have good character is to always make sure that you are honest, honorable and forthright. Make sure there is no implication of dishonesty in any form.

You should also seek to be considerate of others and conscientious in your work. This doesn't mean that you need to be perfect, but it does mean that you are trying to be someone of high character.

Finally, being courageous enough to take a stand to help those in need or to try something new builds character.

Summary

You need to be honest and reliable. You need to be responsible and courageous. Your reputation affects how people deal with you. Having good character results in respect from others and greater self-esteem. Having character requires a constant effort.

Being Valuable

Being liked, admired, important or valuable in school is something most students want. You must realize that others want the same thing. You achieve your goal by doing things others appreciate. It is worth your while to try to be valuable to those with whom you deal.

What you want
It is a good feeling to know you are liked, admired, valuable or important to others.

By other students
You probably want to be liked and admired by your friends and fellow students. If you were part of a team or group, you'd like to be accepted and considered an important member.

By teachers
Since part of the grades you get depends in your relationship with your teacher, you probably want to be liked and respected by your teachers.

By parents
Obviously, you want to feel your parents love you and that you are important to them.

What others want
The people you deal with have things they want in their relationship with you. What they want is similar to what you want and makes you feel good in the relationship.

Personal Improvement

Teachers
Teachers feel happy and satisfied if the students in their classes behave, pay attention, learn and do well in class. They also enjoy having a friendly relationship with their students.

Other students
Your friends and acquaintances enjoy to talk about things of interest, as well as to be involved in fun activities.

Parents
Your parents will feel good and be proud of you, if you do well in school. Though, they will still love you, even if you don't do well.

There are extreme cases where kids will try to please their parents too much, such that they don't have a life of their own.

Become valuable
You should take care of yourself to become valuable. A way to get the good feeling of being liked, admired, valuable and important is to provide others what they want. You can get what you want by helping others get what they want.

To teachers
By doing your assignments, behaving and trying to be a good student, your teachers will probably like you, feel you are important to their class and give you better grades.

Of course, trying too hard can backfire. Even teachers can see through the "apple-polisher" or person who patronizes the teacher in hopes of getting better grades.

Be aware of the teacher's needs, but yet be your own person.

To other students
By having the same interests as your friends and other students, you will be liked. If you do things outstanding, you may be admired. Some kids have the looks, personality or such that they are desired as a friend.

Kids who try too hard to be liked often are scorned. You need to know what interests the other students or find others who are interested in what you like.

Conflict

A problem is that the other kids can dislike a student who plays up to the teacher too much. Sometimes talking back to the teachers and goofing-off in class can win the admiration of fellow classmates. They like someone who isn't afraid and rebels. The problem is that grades can suffer by that behavior.

It is good to try to keep your teacher happy to a degree, but don't do it so much that you alienate the other kids. A little rebellion is fine, but you also must make sure you don't screw up your grades.

Summary

You want to be liked, admired, important and valuable in school. Others want the same thing. You achieve your goal by doing things others appreciate. It is worthwhile to try to be valuable to others.

Personal Improvement

Characteristics of Hyperactive Students

Some students have difficulty paying attention in class, act restless and seem impulsive. They exhibit various characteristics that can be bothersome to teachers, other students and even themselves. In extreme cases, this type of behavior is called Attention Deficit Hyperactivity Disorder or ADHD.

You may have some of these behavior traits or perhaps you know of others who have them.

Short attention span

If you have problems paying attention is easily distracted in class, you may have a short attention span. This is not uncommon among those who watch television a lot. Also, a short attention span may be related a lack of interest in the subject matter.

It is possible to have your lack of attention go to an extreme. In such a case, you may often look about the classroom instead of at the teacher or chalkboard. You may not read directions or follow instructions and then make silly mistakes. Some students with this problem are often forgetful and often lose things necessary for doing tasks. Others are very disorganized.

Also, when in a conversation, you may not pay attention to what the other person is saying and seem rude or uncaring. It takes a lot of self-discipline for you to be able to maintain attention.

Impulsive

Some students are impulsive, blurting out answers before questions have been completed.

Personal Improvement

You may even have difficulty waiting for your turn and often interrupt or intrude upon others. You also may try to dominate activities, interfere in what others are doing, or quit a game or activity before it's done. You also may often be disorganized and fail to plan ahead.

If this is the case, you need to learn to control your impulsive nature and make it useful to you.

Hyperactive

To add to the problem of having a short attention span and being impulsive, some students are also hyperactive. These students often get restless sitting in class and may fidget with their hands or feet or squirm in their seats. They may also talk excessively.

If you have difficulty engaging in activities quietly and even act as if you are driven by a motor, you may have this problem. This is called Attention Deficit Hyperactivity Disorder or ADHD. People are not sure what exactly causes the problem—whether it is medical, genetic or behavioral—but it seems that boys have the disorder more than girls.

If you have this type of excess energy, it can be managed and harnessed into something productive.

Summary

Some students have a short attention span to an extreme, where they even have problems paying attention in a conversation. Other students may also be impulsive. If they also are hyperactive, they may have a condition called Attention Deficit Hyperactivity Disorder or ADHD.

If you may have some of these behavior traits or perhaps you know of others who have them, it is good to try to harness that energy and creativity to become a champion in school and in life.

Harness Your Hyperactivity

Do you often make silly mistakes in a test or your homework because you are rushing through it too fast? Do you also find yourself easily getting distracted, or does your mind go at top speed, jumping from one subject? Are you considered hyperactive?

It is surprising how many students have a short attention span and are considered as hyperactive. Such a condition can be a problem if it is not managed, but it also is energy that can be harnessed to your benefit.

The solution is not difficult, but it does take a fair amount of self-discipline. This lesson will answer the following questions you may have:

- What are some of the characteristics of a hyperactive person, to see if it applies to me?

- What are the benefits of harnessing this energy? What are the possible consequences if it isn't controlled?

- What are some ways to harness or control my energy?

- What examples are there of people who have done this?

If you have some of these traits, this lesson will explain methods to help harness your energy, so you can become a champion in school and get better grades.

Personal Improvement

Characteristics of a hyperactive person

Some students have difficulty paying attention in class, act hyperactive or impulsive. They exhibit various characteristics that can be bothersome to teachers, other students and even themselves. You may have some of these behavior traits or perhaps you know of others who have them.

Have short attention span

Students who have problems paying attention are easily distracted. They may often look about the classroom instead of at the teacher or chalkboard. Such students may not read directions or follow instructions and then make silly mistakes. Some are forgetful and often lose things necessary for doing tasks. Others are very disorganized.

When in a conversation, such a student may not pay attention to what the other person is saying and seem rude or uncaring. It takes a lot of self-discipline for such a person to be able to maintain attention.

Are hyperactive

Hyperactive students often get restless sitting in class and may fidget with their hands or feet or squirm in their seats. They may have difficulty engaging in activities quietly and even act as if they are driven by a motor. They also may talk excessively.

This type of excess energy needs to be managed and harnessed into something productive.

Are impulsive

Some students are impulsive, blurting out answers before questions have been completed. Such students may even have difficulty waiting for their turn and often interrupt or intrude upon others. They also may dominate activities, interfere in what others are doing, or quit a game or activity before it's done.

Such students are also often disorganized and fail to plan ahead. They need to learn to control their impulsive nature and make it useful.

Can excel if hyperactivity is managed

Students who learn to manage or control their hyperactive behavior and to harness that energy and creativity can excel in school, their social life and their careers.

These students have the energy and drive to accomplish many things at once, while other students are struggling to do one thing at a time. Hyperactive or impulsive students are often more curious, which causes them to be easily distracted. They can be more creative, because their mind is always searching for different possibilities and ideas.

Many leaders and entrepreneurs who start their own businesses were once considered hyperactive. Through great self-discipline they were able to control their excessive behaviors and transform them into the energy and creativity needed for greatness.

Consequences of uncontrolled behavior

Students who don't learn to manage hyperactive behavior may suffer unpleasant consequences in school and later in life. See if you recognize some of these consequences.

Silly mistakes can mean poor grades

Students who are hyperactive and don't pay attention may be prone to make silly mistakes in tests or homework. They may forget to do required assignments or even do the wrong one. Also, they may often lose their homework, books, or other necessary items.

Can irritate people

Inattention, hyperactivity, or impulsiveness can result in serious social problems. Some students can irritate teachers and fellow students by talking out of turn in class, answering someone else's question, or simply being disruptive in class.

Personal Improvement

People don't like always being interrupted. Such students may end up getting poor grades and not having many—or any—friends. Such behavioral excesses can make it difficult to make and keep friendships.

Don't get good jobs
Later on in their lives, this uncontrolled behavior can result in them not getting the good jobs or pay that they should, according to their intellectual ability or skills. They may even lose their jobs due to poor job performance, attention and organizational problems, or relationship difficulties. Other times, they may simply quit out of boredom.

Can get depressed
Problems in this area can lead to loneliness, low self-esteem and depression.

But don't get discouraged, if you had some of these excessive behaviors. There are ways to harness your energy productively.

Ways to control and harness your energy
Following are some ideas on how to control your tendency to get distracted, to make silly mistakes, or to be hyperactive or impulsive and to turn that energy into creative and useful forces:

1. First of all, get motivated to improve yourself

2. Next, be aware of what you do that causes problems

3. Then, use tricks to harness your energy

4. Finally, acknowledge your good behavior

Get motivated to improve yourself
Identify your areas of strength. By focusing on these areas, you can develop the confidence and skills to tackle other, difficult situations. If you realize the consequences of being impulsive or forgetful, then you can be motivated to use some tricks to manage your forgetfulness.

You must make a commitment to adapt your behavior and set a goal of increased performance. You must attempt to manage inappropriate or damaging behavior.

Who wants to always goof up or to feel that people don't like you? It is tough to change, but if you feel you have such a problem, you just have to set your mind on controlling yourself.

Be aware of what you do that causes problems
Be aware of behavior you don't think is good, that causes problems for you, or that turns off other people. Are there things you seem to be always doing—like losing things or getting bored? Do other students seem not to like to talk to you? Are you always interrupting other people when they are talking?

Analyze what you do and perhaps make a list of some of these traits that may be causing you trouble. Once you are aware of what you are doing, it is much easier to correct your problems and to improve the way you act.

Use tricks to harness your energy
There are a number of ideas to try to harness your energy and to control any excessive behavior you may have.

Break projects into small parts
Since you are able to do several things at once, use that ability to your advantage. If you have a large project to do, break it into little pieces and do several of those smaller tasks at once—making sure you complete each of them. This way, you don't get bored or sidetracked from the larger project, and soon the little, completed pieces will add up to the whole project being completed.

Personal Improvement

If you can complete several things at once, be proud of the fact. Juggle your activities effectively, but don't let things go undone.

Take notes in class, along with ideas
In class, you can take notes of the important facts that the teacher is explaining. This skill is very useful when you are in college. But since your mind is so active, assign an area on your notepaper for other ideas, inventions, doodles or such. You may have to let your teacher what you are doing, so she doesn't think you are goofing around. Or at least be careful about it.

I remember when I was in the 7th grade, I took down notes what the teacher was saying, but I also wrote ideas and doodled in the columns of my notepaper. When my teacher saw that I had drawings of Superman and fast cars on my notepaper, he showed my notes to the class to try to embarrass me. I just learned to be more careful with this teacher. I still got an A in the class.

Let others know
People like to help those who want to improve. If you have been having trouble because you are somewhat hyperactive, you can let your teachers, parents and friends know you are trying to manage and control being impulsive. This may be very hard to do, and it depends on how others will respond. At the very least, they should think more of you for trying to rectify any problems.

Although, some may want to give advice, that can also be boring.

Answering questions in class or in discussions
Be careful not to dominate the discussion all the time. Cool it once in a while. Try to be considerate of others and let them give their opinions. It is tough to force yourself to listen to others and to pay attention, but it is a skill you should perfect. People don't like those who only talk and don't listen.

Taking tests
Thoroughly prepare for test. Try to be methodical. Learn to read faster, so you don't miss important information.

Doing homework
Do several things at once, preferably two different subjects. Watching TV and doing homework is not too effective, although some students can talk on the phone or listen to the radio and still do their homework.

Give yourself a pat on the back
Pat yourself on the back when you complete a task or avoid a distraction When you catch yourself doing something negative, tell yourself the correct behavior, but don't put yourself down.

Success stories
The following are some stories of people who exhibited these traits and learned to control them, thus resulting in their success.

Tom Hopkins
Hopkins dropped out of college, because it was too boring. He talked a mile-a-minute and ran around like a madman. This turned people off to him. Soon his parents told him they would still love him, even though he was doomed to be a failure.

He put his mind to controlling his energy. He controlled his rapid talking and his actions and soon became a top salesman. He later started to speak to groups on sales and gave motivational speeches around the country. He has also written several books about selling and is considered quite successful.

Brian Tracey
Tracey thought he was very smart, and he would argue and interrupt his friends in school. But soon he realized that he didn't have that many friends, and the reason was that he was always interrupting them and blurting out his opinions before they could finish what they had to say.

He then worked being more considerate, listening to what others had to say and on improving his personality. He is now a successful businessman in Canada.

Personal Improvement

Others

Do you know of any other examples of people who have harnessed their energy to excel in school and become happy and successful people?

Summary

Examine yourself. If you have some of these characteristics, think about correcting them, so you won't be making silly mistakes in school and turning off other people in the process.

Harness your energy and creativity and become a champion in school and in life.

Feedback on Hyperactivity

Students from around the world send email to the *School for Champions* with questions and comments on various aspects of getting good grades in school. The following letters concern being hyperactive. Note that the letters have not been edited for correct grammar or spelling.

Has a nervous condition

Question
August 8

I came to know from your website that I am a Hyperactive personality. This is the possible cause of my nervous behaviour. I have been a nervous personality throughout my life. But could not realise what could be the possible cause of my nervous behaviour. Now I know it is because I am hyperactive. I am working on this.

Thanks to you for helping me figure out the solution to my personality disorder.

Navin - **India**

Answer
Being hyperactive certainly can cause a person to seem nervous. But someone can be nervous from pushing too hard and trying to do too much. Everyone needs to take a break and enjoy the world around him or her.

I am glad you are on the way to improving yourself. But do not think of it as a personality disorder. In fact, think that you are lucky you are this way, because when you are able to have more control over your nervousness, you should be a special person. Best wishes in being a champion.

Personal Improvement

Has hyperactive son

Question
July 29

I have a five-year-old son. He is very hyperactive. But he is very smart for his age. You can get him to do the work, but a one point he seem to cannot keep still. I also notice he does not take following directions good at times. Some times he can be good than 85% of the time his behavior is horrible. His teacher even said to me that this may interfere with his learning. What can I do as a mother to get him to relax and take things slow?

Vandora - **USA**

Answer
Boys that age always seem to be squirming and moving about. Sometimes they hear the directions, even if they don't seem to be listening. But paying attention to the wrong things can result in not listening.

Playing outside is much better to burn off excess energy than watching TV. At home, giving him a little extra love and a hug can often calm a child down.

A smart child often needs many things to stimulate the mind. Some children and adults are thinking of several things at one time. Learning to focus can be a chore.

I hope these ideas help. I am sure your son will do fine.

Gets bored in class

Question
September 16

I think its a good article, but at the same time I am a college student who is hyperactive and it's hard to get motivated in the classroom or like what we are doing because all we do is sit and the teacher talks and I quickly lose interest.

Do you have any suggestions, because I don't mean to rude to my teachers but I very much dislike the classroom atmosphere of sitting all day.

Amy - **USA**

Answer
Good teachers have interaction with the students. But many just lecture. That can be very boring.

If the material the teacher is presenting is important, taking notes is a good way to keep interested. But also, you can have a second page in the notebook, where you are writing down other thoughts or working on other homework. In this way, you can do two things at once, but yet keep in tune enough just in case you are asked a question.

Taking notes in class is a good practice in college in any case.

One thing to remember is that you (or your parents) are paying for your education. You want to get your money's worth and learn things that are useful to you or are required to get a degree. So, trying things to make the class more interesting or to at least get stuff done is in your best interests.

Personal Improvement

On the other hand, if you don't like the classroom atmosphere, perhaps you should get into something more physical that you like to do. Get some plans for the future and move in the direction that suits you best. I hope these ideas help, and best wishes in what you do.

Article helped understanding

Question
May 1

I am a 10th grade student and have had difficulty throughout my junior high and high school times. I was diagnosed with A.D.D. about two years ago and have found the medication I have tried to be ineffective or even make me feel depressed. Reading your article on how to Harness Your Hyperactivity really helped me better understand my condition and made me feel better about myself. A couple days ago I have moved on my problem and contacted my counselor and notified my parents. I am starting to go down the right road. I just wanted to thank you for your information. Have a nice day.

Miles - **USA**

Answer
I'm glad the material was useful to you and am excited that you are on your way to overcome your challenges and become a champion.

Best wishes in your endeavors and keep me informed on your progress.

Section 9: Summary

You've now learned how to get good grades. You've been given some ideas of how to do your homework more effectively, how to prepare for tests and do well on your exams, and how to deal with teachers. You've also seen some special skills that can help you in school, how to learn more effectively, and how to apply a positive philosophy in school and in life.

We hope these ideas will prove helpful to you, such that you will become a champion in school and move on to better and greater things. Not only do we hope you will succeed, we know you have it in you to move to the top.

Summary

Ron Kurtus

Ron Kurtus is the founder of the *School for Champions*, an award-winning educational website that not only provides basic academic lessons and strategies for success, but also encourages positive attitudes and service to others. Over 500,000 lessons are accessed each month.

The series of lessons that provides strategies to succeed in school is *Tricks for Good Grades*, which is the basis for this book. Hundreds of students have sent in letters, asking for advice or expressing their views on school issues. A small portion of those letters and their answers are included in the book.

Ron has a wide range of interests, many of which are expressed in lessons in the *School for Champions*. You can access the site at: **www.school-for-champions.com**.

Summary

Index

A
Achieve your goals 139
ADHD 176
Admirable traits 167
Admired 171
Afraid to speak 119
angry teacher 75
Apologize for cheating 22
attention span 175
Attitude of speed 27

B
Be Good at Tests 47
Be prepared for trouble 111
Become valuable 172
Being liked 171
Benefits of being excellent 153
Benefits of cheating 10
Benefits of good health 146

C
Can't excel 162
Can't read fast 99
Can't read well 105
Can't remember 65
Celebrate 143

Champion 2, 139
Champion attitude 141
Championship teams 54
Championship teams prepare 63
Character 142, 167
Cheat on the SATS 13
Cheated on math 20
Cheating 9, 142
Cheating not contagious 15
Cheating yourself 18
Cheating, feedback 13
class brain 130
Common sense 15
Competing with friend 52
Complex reading 96
Comprehension 95
Confidence 107, 141, 153
Confident 151
Confused about speed reading 102
Consequences of cheating 10
Courage 167
Cramming 54

D
Determination 142
Discipline 38

Index

Distracted 177
Do homework effectively 6
Does bad on tests 71
Doesn't interest me 39
Drinking alcohol 147
Drinks 55
Drugs 147

E
Emotional health 145
encouragement 75
Energy 142
Esteem 153
Excel in tests 53
Excellence 142
Excellence, feedback 155
Excellent 153
Excess energy 178
Exercise 55

F
Fake it 6
Fear you will forget 107
Feel confident 112
Feel guilty 23
Find out about teachers 79
Focus on allotted time 28
Foreign students, reading 103
forgetful 175
Freezes up in tests 69
Friend might copy 42
Friends cheat 21
Fun to cheat 14

G
Get Homework Done 31
Get it done 29
Get some support 140
Give thanks 143
Goes blank 67
Good at taking tests 51
Good character 167
Good grades 3
Good teacher 79
Good teachers 73
Goofing up tests 61

Got an F 66
Grades depend on test scores 45
Grading unfairly 84
Grouping words 97

H
Harness energy 177
Harness your energy 180
Have some fun 27
Health, feedback 149
Healthy 145
Highlighter 93
Homework 5, 25
Homework amount 80
Homework boring 40
Homework in morning 41
Homework with Friends 33
Homework with friends 32
Homework, feedback 37
Honesty 167
honesty 142
How much time 28
How not to be nervous 117
Hyperactive mind 31
Hyperactive Students 175
Hyperactivity 177
Hyperactivity, feedback 185

I
I like cheating 14
I'm a cheater 17
Importance of grade 58
Improve your memory 94
Impulsive 175, 178
Instant messaging 34
interesting teacher 81
Interrupt 178
Irritate people 179

K
Keep focused 31
Know subject matter 108
Know your speech 109
Knowledge level 58
Knowledgeable 151

Index

L
Lack of knowledge 151
Lazy 11, 37
Learn from observation 129
Learning 127
Liked by teacher 90
Listen to music 32
losers 130
low profile 77
Lunch detention 86

M
Manage your time 31
mean teacher 75
Memory 94
Mental concentration 32
Mental health 146
Mental process 57
Morally bankrupt 11
Motivated 53, 181
Motivates self 115
motivating 75
Motivation 141
Music 32

N
Negative attitudes 62
Nervous before speaking 116
Nervous condition 185
Not motivated 43
Note taking 91

O
Observing Others 129
Organizing your time 91
Others make fun of me 114
Overcome fears of speaking 108
Overconfident 54, 61

P
Pace yourself 32
Pain from concentrating 100
Parents feel good 172
Parents put on pressure 20
personality conflict 76
Personality traits 15

Plan of action 140
Poor attitudes 61
Poor grades 156
Practice speech 109
Practice taking tests 49
Practice with homework 51
Practicing taking tests 51
Praise 154
Preparation 63
Prepare for test 48
Prepare mentally 53
Preparing for test 59
Preparing physically 55
Preparing your knowledge 54
Presentations 118
pressure to cheat 9
Problem solving study 54
Procrastinates 43
Proper mental state 58
Pros and cons of cheating 9

R
Read faster 93
Read rapidly 28
Reading boring material 113
Reading faster 95
Reading, feedback 99
Rebelling 18
Recall better 133
Reduce fear of audience 110
Refresh body 59
Refresh mental state 59
Refresh your body 57
Relationship with teacher 171
Respectful to teacher 7
Responsibility 167
Ron Kurtus 191

S
Sample tests 52
School for Champions 2, 191
Scores 5
Set a time limit 35
Setting your goal 139
Sexually harassing 89
Short attention span 178

Index

Should you cheat 11
Sidetracked 31
Silly mistakes 61, 177
Skilled 151
Skim reading 96
Skip homework 27
Sleep 55
Slow learner 156
Smoking 147
Social studying 33
Socializing 25
Solitary studying 33
Sound words while reading 104
Speak in front your class 107
Speaking, feedback 113
Special homework skills 28
Special skills 91
Steps to take 63
Stressed out 65
Students cheat 19
study habits 130
study methods 33
Study techniques 151
Studying for test 59
Stuttering 121
Suddenly fearful 124
Sugar 55
Switch subjects 32

T
Teacher is a Jerk 75
Teacher nags 85
Teacher picks on me 86, 87
Teacher relationship 6
Teacher sexually harassing 89
Teachers 73
Teachers don't care 13
Teachers, feedback 83
Teaching others 133
Television 32
Tell the teacher 16
Test anxiety 48
Test not important 62
Test scores 5
Tests 45, 51
Tests, feedback 65

test-taking skill 47
Time yourself 28
Troublemaker when speaking 111

U
Uncontrolled behavior 179
Underestimate difficulty 62
Understand what you read 93
Using notes in speaking 110

V
Valuable 171
verbalizing 133
Verify knowledge in a test 45

W
winners 130
Work too slow 48
Worry about tests 45

Z
Zip through Homework 27
Zipping not the best 38

LaVergne, TN USA
18 October 2010
201307LV00001B/31/P